STRUGGLES OVER THE WORD

RACE AND RELIGION IN
O'CONNOR,
FAULKNER,
HURSTON,
AND
WRIGHT

Struggles Over the Word

Race and Religion in O'Connor, Faulkner, Hurston, and Wright

By
Timothy P. Caron

Mercer
University
Press
2000

ISBN 0-86554-669-X
MUP/H498

© 2000 Mercer University Press
6316 Peake Road
Macon, Georgia 31210-3960
All rights reserved

First Edition.

The paper used in this publication meets
the minimum requirements of American
National Standard for Information
Sciences—Permanence of Paper for
Printed Library Materials,
ANSI Z39.48-1984.

CIP is available from the Library of Congress

TABLE OF CONTENTS

ACKNOWLEDGMENTS

W HEN I PICK up a scholarly work, I always turn to the Acknowledgements page first. Reading the names of the people to whom the author gives praise and recognition reminds me of the truth of what I tell my students: writing, at its best, is a collaborative process. Of course, there are lots of lonely, anguished hours in front of an infuriating blinking cursor, but there are also moments of pure joy derived from the exchange and interaction of ideas and shared experience.

I'd like to thank the following people for their help in shepherding this book through its many iterations. Thanks to *Studies in American Fiction* and *The Southern Quarterly* for their permission to reprint essays which later became chapters four and five of this book. Rick Moreland was the first reader of this material, and in many ways, he remains my best reader. He continues to be a role-model of the teacher-scholar and a sartorial inspiration for me. Scott Peeples, Paul Buchanan, and Kathleen Fitzpatrick also read the entire manuscript, even when they had lots of other work to do, and I appreciate all of their good advice. There aren't enough fish tacos to express my gratitude to them. I'd also like to thank all of my colleagues in the English Department and the College of Liberal Arts at California State University, Long Beach, for creating an environment of mutual respect and collegiality. Many thanks also to my students for their energy, enthusiasm and willingness to explore the intertwined issues of race and religion in our classrooms. Southern California ain't the South, but it's not so bad, after all. Finally, I'd like to thank my best collaborator, my wife, Shea Caron. She makes everything possible.

To my mom, Carol Caron, who taught me the power of stories, ensured I was "raised right," and made me go to Sunday School.

This whole book is but a draft—nay, but the draft of a draft.
Oh, Time, Strength, Cash, and Patience!

Herman Melville
Moby Dick

STRUGGLES OVER THE WORD

RACE AND RELIGION IN
O'CONNOR,
FAULKNER,
HURSTON,
AND
WRIGHT

CHAPTER ONE

"HOW DARE YOU PREACH TO ME ABOUT YOUR INFERNAL BIBLE!": STRUGGLES OVER THE WORD

Each writer writes the missing parts to the other writer's story.
— Alice Walker

All scripture is given by inspiration of God, and is profitable for doctrine, for reproof, for correction, for instruction in righteous-ness: That the man of God may be perfect, thoroughly furnished unto all good works.
— II Timothy 3:16-17[1]

THE SOUTH IS a battlefield, a site of struggle for interpretive control over the Bible. In America, the Bible has been used to both condone and condemn slavery and institutionalized racism. Southern whites turned to the Bible to justify their racism and/or often ignored those passages which spoke of equality or liberation for all of God's children. African-American churches, on the other

---

[1] All scriptural quotes throughout this study are from the King James translation of the Bible.

hand, frequently turned to those stories which seemed to promise a deliverance from the social ills of slavery and, later, Jim Crow. This study investigates the Bible and, just as importantly, its attendant interpretive institutions and discourses as intertextual sources in selected white and black Southern writers: Flannery O'Connor's *Wise Blood*, William Faulkner's *Light in August*, Zora Neale Hurston's *Moses, Man of the Mountain*, and Richard Wright's *Uncle Tom's Children*.

All of these texts engage in a larger cultural dialogue. O'Connor acknowledged William Faulkner as the central figure of Southern literature, and she recognized the sometimes cramped space that Southern authors are forced to share because of his imposing figure. In "The Grotesque in Southern Fiction," she wrote, "I think the writer is initially set going by literature more than by life.... The presence alone of Faulkner in our midst makes a great difference in what the writer can and cannot permit himself to do. Nobody wants his mule and wagon stalled on the same track the Dixie Limited is roaring down."[2] However, these texts and their authors not only dialogue among themselves in acknowledged ways (Faulkner and O'Connor, or Wright and Hurston) but also in previously unacknowledged ways (Hurston and Faulkner, O'Connor and Wright) *and* with the region's pervasive discursive practices, especially as they are manifested in differing approaches to reading the Bible. Studying the relationships in and among white and black Southern authors' intertextual relationships to the Bible should help to end the debilitating and artificial segregation that still exists within the discipline of Southern literary studies. Literary works are sign-systems which participate in larger, cultural discursive practices. Therefore, neither O'Connor, Faulkner, Hurston, nor Wright "escapes the cultural web"[3] of Southern race and religion. In fact,

---

[2] Flannery O'Connor, "The Grotesque in Southern Fiction," 45.

[3] Michel Grisset, "Introduction: Faulkner Between the Texts," 3.

this cultural web binds them all together—touching the web in one location sends ripples throughout the whole.

One of the goals of this project is to contribute to the on-going negotiations of just what it is we mean when we use phrases such as "Southern literature" and "Southern studies." Despite the spate of recent anthologies and critical studies which attempt to view the South in its racial complexity, Thadious Davis's observation in "Expanding the Limits: The Intersection of Race and Region" that "whites in the South became simply 'Southerners' without a racial designation, but blacks in the South became simply 'blacks' without a regional designation"[4] still largely holds true. Faulkner and O'Connor, for instance, are widely designated *Southern* writers, and Hurston and Wright are categorized as black authors. Whereas women writers have been given grudging admission to the club of Southern literature, exclusion along color lines has been stronger. Despite anthologies such as *Black Southern Voices*, *The Literature of the American South*, and *The Oxford Book of the American South* and critical studies such as *The History of Southern Literature*, *Southern Literature and Literary Theory*, and *The Future of Southern Letters*, all of which call for the integration of Southern studies, the separation of race and region that Davis observed a decade ago still generally holds true. Hurston and Wright are only beginning to be considered in terms of region. It is time to move beyond simply calling for an integrated study of the South's literary culture and actually begin to sketch out what the new landscape will look like.

"...knowledge hitherto unextracted..."

AS STUDENTS OF Southern studies have long known, "race" is a central concern of the region's literature. However, because of the

---

4 Thadious Davis, "Expanding the Limits: The Intersection of Race and Region," 4.

division between Southern literature and African-American literary studies, Faulkner or Robert Penn Warren's concern with race, for instance, was rarely juxtaposed with, say, Alice Walker's concern with race. How might we frame the question so that both black and white Southerners' voices could be heard on the issue? In his essay, "American Parapedagogy for 2000 and Beyond: Intertextual, International, Industrial Strength," Charles Vandersee encourages us as teachers of American literature to adopt a pedagogy of intertextuality which does more than "'make links' among texts."[5] An intertextual approach recognizes, among other things, that "texts taken collectively have knowledge hitherto unextracted, and major knowledge at that, which becomes revealed only as texts are pushed together rather than simply juxtaposed."[6] Vandersee's essay is directed toward the more general audience of American literature scholars, but the principle is especially suggestive of strategies for new approaches to Southern literary studies. He lists nineteen possible American "Texts" (all of them could be fruitful in a Southern literature class) which could form the basis for investigations of our national literature, such as sameness versus diversity; hopes for prosperity; ethnicity; movement/motion/transportation; and American practicality, just to name a few. No list can pretend to be exhaustive; however, conspicuous in its absence is any mention of the Bible, or any of the other religious texts that have contributed to the creation of American literature. Vandersee's otherwise excellent essay reflects, I think, a common oversight in American literary studies. As Jenny Franchot has noticed, "this neglect may reflect how unimportant religion is in the lives of literary scholars.... Such narrowness...is especially ruinous in our field, since America has been and continues to be manifestly religious in

---

5 Charles Vandersee, "American Parapedagogy for 2000 and Beyond: Intertextual, International, Industrial Strength," 413.
6 Ibid, 415.

complex and intriguing ways. And not only America but American literature."[7] Franchot's words, as do Vandersee's, hold a particular importance for the study of Southern literature because of the crucial role religion has played in the South. In "Faulkner Between the Texts," Michel Grisset comments on the richest source of intertextual borrowing in American literature: "The Bible (itself admittedly an intertextual nexus) may be considered as a well-nigh inextinguishable source of intertextuality in the field of English and American literature: the biblical connection is even one of the most outstanding characteristics of American literature."[8] Given America's involvement in dissident Protestantism since its earliest settlement, such a claim suggests a reading strategy or orientation to use in reading our national literature. Grisset's statement holds particular promise for the study of Southern literature because, while the South's churches certainly were not homogenous (by race or by class), the region remains more firmly rooted in a tradition of personal Bible study than any other in our country.

The common ground shared by O'Connor, Faulkner, Hurston, and Wright are the same intertwined concerns shared by most of the rest of the South, both white and black: race and religion. Race and religion, especially the region's concerns over interpreting the Bible, form the intertextual network that binds such seemingly disparate texts together, and, as Jonathan Culler reminds us, intertextual reading "leads one to think of a text as a dialogue with other texts, an act of absorption, parody and criticism."[9] In the on-going dialogue between the four texts considered here and their larger, common milieu, *Wise Blood* demonstrates one common white Southern response to politics' "intrusion" into religion by

---

[7] Jenny Franchot, "Invisible Domain: Religion and American Literary Studies," 839.

[8] Grisset, "Introduction: Faulkner Between the Texts," 3.

[9] Jonathan Culler, "Presupposition and Intertextuality," 1383.

emphasizing the need for individual redemption, stressing the continued viability of Christian salvation over "political" questions such as race. *Light in August* displays an antagonism toward the manifestations of a Southern tradition of racist biblical interpretation, while *Moses, Man of the Mountain* responds to the white South's hateful appropriations of the Bible by asserting that God's Word also contains powerful models for constructing an affirming African-American community. *Uncle Tom's Children* contributes to the cultural dialogue by illustrating how to use biblical discourse to politically mobilize these communities. As reflected in their biblical revoicings, these works display the Protestant concerns of redemption, salvation, and regeneration which are central to both the white and black churches of the South. Furthermore, these texts reveal some of the shifting boundaries of Southern scriptural interpretation—white evangelical efforts to shout down those who would introduce "extraneous concerns" like politics into biblical interpretation; conservative white unease regarding biblical interpretation; black communal pride and/or militancy.

While all four authors' fiction argues for the centrality of the Bible in both the black and white Southern experience, each offers a different viewpoint on how this iconic text has shaped Southern society and its fiction. Political, racial, and religious differences influence the way each work revoices the Bible, while the South's violence reverberates throughout each text's biblical appropriations. For example, *Wise Blood* insists that an apostate South must violently forsake this world's concerns and concentrate instead on the necessity of personal, spiritual regeneration. *Light in August* critiques the white South's biblical justifications for brutal racial violence like the lynching of Joe Christmas. *Moses, Man of the Mountain* insists upon constructing a sustaining African-American community as an antidote to this racially motivated violence, while *Uncle Tom's Children* demands the mobilizing of the black church to help overturn Jim Crow policies.

Within this colloquy, all of these works appeal to the Bible's apparently common language, the text which, in many ways, authorizes the South's dominant discourse and informs many of the society's central concerns, such as its dominant religiosity, race relations, and rhetoric. Despite the common invocation of this authorizing text, each writer's fiction makes its appeal in a different and often conflicting manner. The cultural conversation's recurring topic is violence—violent metaphors of Christian conversion, brutal lynchings to preserve and justify Jim Crow, vehement differences over biblical interpretation and what passages interpretive communities emphasize, and fierce refusals to live by the dehumanizing strictures of Southern racism. Violence marks the spaces within the South's "cultural dialogue" where sharp divisions occur, and these divisions correspond to the region's struggle for interpretive control of the Bible.

What occurs in this inter(textual)play is a re-examining of the South's intertwining of race and religion. O'Connor's Hazel Motes and Enoch Emery embody, respectively, the white South's evangelical emphasis upon personal salvation and the tragic consequences of unregenerate man's animal-like existence. Faulkner's Joe Christmas demonstrates the life-and-death stakes of biblical interpretation in the South. Hurston follows a long established black folk tradition in appropriating the Old Testament Moses to teach lessons of community pride and self-worth. And Wright creates tactical alliances between the black church and the American Communist Party, forcing us to re-examine the Bible as a text concerned with social justice. At the conclusion of each text, we are forced by the biblical intertexts to reread the Bible through new eyes. Is self-mutilation too high a price for spiritual regeneration? How did the white South interpret the story of Noah and his son, Ham, as a justification for slavery? How did Moses become the cornerstone of an African-American "liberation theology?" What tactical alliances are possible between Christianity and social justice movements? These biblical rewritings reveal the ways in which, despite the strident claims of Southern fundamentalists, the Bible is not a transparent text, but is one which is always interpreted and received in very specific historical circumstances. What differences might appear when two texts evoke the same preceding intertext? Despite "redistributing" particular "bits of code, formulae, rhythmic models, fragments of social languages"[10] from a common source text, what is revealed in the differences in O'Connor, Faulkner, Hurston, and Wright's evocations of the same Bible?

Reading the Bible in the Bible Belt

TO USE FLANNERY O'Connor's phrase, the South was—and to a large extent, still is—a "Christ-haunted" region. It is haunted because it has long been under the virtually hegemonic religious control of Protestant denominations—both black and white—that stress the need for personal salvation and require an individual, close reading and knowledge of the Scriptures after this conversion. A 1906 religious census of the white South, east of the Mississippi River and excepting Kentucky, revealed that 96.6 percent of the population was Protestant and 90 percent were Baptist and Methodist.[11] This numerical and theological dominance has continued in the white South, at least until as recently as the 1960s when "membership in Baptist and Methodist

---

[10] Roland Barthes, "Theory of the Text," 39.
[11] Samuel S. Hill, *The South and the North in American Religion*, 110.

churches constituted nearly 80% of the total church affiliation" in the Deep South.[12]

These dominant Protestant sects, along with the Presbyterians, which number a distant third,[13] gained ascendancy in the South beginning with the revivals that swept through the South in the very early 1800s. This "Great Revival," as it was called, turned the white South away from its Episcopal/Church of England roots and toward the denominations that still control it today. Success in proselytizing their Episcopal neighbors, whose churches were seen as being too liturgical, can be attributed to the heightened emotional appeals and emphasis upon sin of the Baptist and Methodist churches.[14] Also, after the American Revolution, Baptists and Methodists had none of the taint of the "establishment" that still lingered over their Anglican brothers.[15]

The Great Revival swept across Tennessee and Kentucky, moved through the South between 1801 and 1805, and solidified white Southern evangelical dominance, achieving a powerful majority by 1810. According to Samuel S. Hill, a type of regional "orthodoxy in religion" became evident by 1830.[16] In *Southern Churches in Crisis*, Hill proclaims that the "diversities within

---

[12] Wayne J. Flynt, "One in the Spirit, Many in the Flesh: Southern Evangelicals," 23.

To speak of a unified, and univocal, black or white church in the 1990s would be a gross inaccuracy considering the increasingly diverse religious profile of the region. However, the phrase "white church" will be used to describe a cluster of denominations—usually Baptist, Methodist, and Presbyterian—that continue to contain the majority of the white South's believers. By the same token, the phrase "black church" serves as a sort of historical short-hand to describe the black Christian church that arose from Christian missionary efforts in the South and the "invisible" slave church of the antebellum period.

[13] Samuel S. Hill, "Survey of Southern Religious History," 388.

[14] John B. Boles, "The Discovery of Southern Religious History," in *Interpreting Southern History*, John B. Boles, ed., 26.

[15] Hill, *South and the North in American Religion*, 24, 21.

[16] Hill, "Survey of Southern Religious History," 395.

Southern Protestantism are minimalized by the striking sameness within and between denominations."[17] Perhaps the most apparent differences among white southern Protestant denominations were class distinctions. Of the major sects, Baptists were held in lowest esteem, usually because of poor, rural memberships, Methodists were a little more respectable, and the Episcopal church was the church of the aristocratic and mannered South. It is interesting to note that Faulkner was christened in the Methodist church as a boy but began occasionally attending Oxford's Episcopal church with his wife Estelle Oldham after he was no longer called "Count No 'Count" and had bought and restored the Rowan Oak estate.

Wayne J. Flynt succinctly characterizes the uniformity of the white Southern churches:

> Appeal was to the heart more than to the head, and conversion was the dominant religious experience. The quest for personal holiness which followed conversion took an individual course; reform was inward and aimed at the individual, not outward and aimed at society. Theology was heavily laced with Calvinistic notions of the sinfulness of man and the need for repentance. Services were less liturgical, reliance on biblical authority more complete, the importance of good, popular preaching greater than was true among other American Protestants.[18]

Without doubt, one could easily rouse a stirring debate among Southern Protestant denominations over questions such as infant baptism or even the scripturally required mode of baptism. However, Flynt and Hill recognize the Bible's role as an iconic book, possessing a central and profound role in the white South's

---

[17] Ibid, 76.
[18] Flynt, "One in the Spirit, Many in the Flesh: Southern Evangelicals," 27-28

religiosity. In fact, Hill, in numbering the common denominators of the "radical wings" which exercised the most control over Southern Protestant denominations, first lists their common call to "maximize" the Bible.[19] That is, the Bible provided the guidelines for their theology and a manual for stewardship after conversion, and a thorough knowledge of it was expected as a result of personal study. Flynt delineates two of the major historical causes of what he calls this "common ideology" of the white Southern church. First, the incredibly popular revivals and camp-meetings, which were extremely inter-denominational and interracial during the Great Revival, effectively propagated this "common ideology." Second, only a small minority of churches had full-time, one-vocation ministers, so weekly preaching and church-going also overlapped denominations.[20] "The Bible Belt was a well-entrenched stereotype by the early twentieth century," writes David Harrell, Jr., "and it was one with clear substance to it."[21] The theological homogeneity of the white South's church-goers intensified the Protestant concerns of salvation, redemption, and evangelism.

The concern in Southern white churches with personal piety and salvation to the virtual exclusion of concerns over social justice have been well documented by historians of Southern religion, especially Samuel S. Hill's classic study, *Southern Churches in Crisis*. For instance, white church-goers in the South rarely, if ever, heard sermons on social ills such as share-cropping, the chain gang, illiteracy, and certainly not on racial injustice. Instead, generally speaking, the white church adopted two strategies that date back to the antebellum period—silence and capitulation. As the white South anguished over the state of its

---

19 Samuel S. Hill, *Southern Churches in Crisis*, 76.

20 Flynt, "One in the Spirit, Many in the Flesh: Southern Evangelicals," 27, 37.

21 David Harrell, Jr, introduction to *Varieties of Southern Evangelicalism*, 2.

soul, and as divisions deepened between North and South in the decades immediately preceding the Civil War, the white church increasingly sought to justify slavery on biblical grounds. To refute abolitionist claims that slavery denied African-Americans access to the gospel, Southern clergy sought to evangelize the slaves. However, the slavocracy "feared that converted blacks would become unruly servants or might even demand freedom and equality."[22] Undoubtedly, a great deal of the white South's fear of religiously informed slaves stemmed from Nat Turner's revolt in 1831. If slaves were to receive religious instruction, it must of the "proper" kind. The white church became even more complicitous in slavery when its largest denominations split over the issue of slavery—the Methodists in 1844, the Baptists in 1845, and the Presbyterians at the forming of the Confederacy.[23] The white Southern church was now completely aligned with slavery and set about defending the "peculiar institution" on biblical grounds. As Forrest G. Wood has noted, the white Southern church relied upon several biblical texts (or biblical silences) to justify slavery. The ancient Israelites possessed slaves; Jesus makes no pronouncements against slavery in the New Testament; Paul and other New Testament writers admonish slaves to obey their masters—all of this was taken as solid "proof" by the white South that chattel slavery was divinely ordained by God.[24] Much of this same rhetoric survived well into twentieth-century pulpits.

The white South's emphasis upon segregation was bolstered by its theology, which emphasized evangelism over social justice; moreover, the white southern church was devoted to a biblically sanctioned racial segregation. Speaking of the region's most numerous and powerful denomination, Mark Newman

---

[22] Blake Touchstone, "Planters and Slave Religion in the South," 99.

[23] Ibid, 100.

[24] Forrest G. Wood, *The Arrogance of Faith: Christianity and Race in America from the Colonial Era to the Twentieth Century*, 38-111.

characterizes white Baptists in the following manner: "Subsidiary to their devotion to God and scripture, Baptists held primary commitments to evangelism, law and order, peace and stability.... Baptists claimed that Matthew 24:14, the 'Great Commission,' required them to convert 'the lost at home and abroad.' Citing Romans 13:1-2 and Titus 3:1, they insisted that the Bible taught Christians to obey the law. Baptists heralded Jesus as the prince of peace."[25] Jim Crow was the law of the land, and the white South abided by that law. However, in another instance of its twisted logic on race, the white South also relied upon violence and lynchings to make sure that southern blacks maintained their "proper place" in the region's hierarchy and justified this violence on the grounds of maintaining law and order. A grim reminder of this convoluted rationalizing can be found in Henry Smith's "spectacle lynching" in Paris, Texas, in 1893. One of the souvenirs of Smith's murder is a photograph that was sold as a postcard keepsake for those who missed the event. The photo shows a shockingly large crowd around the scaffold, "emblazoned with a large sign that proclaimed 'JUSTICE.'"[26]

Race was a crucial interpretive issue for the white church because it could be construed as a key hermeneutical issue. Both before and after the Civil War, during slavery and Jim Crow, white southern "Christians linked biblical inerrancy to social and cultural practice. Just as slave-holders used the Bible to defend the holding of slaves, twentieth century fundamentalists used it to defend segregation. If they were wrong in their interpretation of the Bible regarding race, then on what other doctrinal or social issues might they be mistaken?"[27] Harriet Jacobs's *Incidents in the*

---

25 Mark Newman, "Southern Baptists and Desegregation, 1945-1980," 182.

26 Grace Elizabeth Hale, *Making Whiteness: The Culture of Segregation in the South, 1890-1940*, 208.

27 Bill J. Leonard, "A Theology for Racism: Southern Fundamentalists and the Civil Rights Movement," 180.

Life of a Slave Girl testifies to the insights of African-Americans into the twisted preachings of the white South. After Nat Turner's insurrection, the community's only black church was shut down, and slaves' religious training was undertaken only under the watchful eyes of white masters. Jacobs recounts a sermon preached by the Reverend Pike, which is a litany of stereotypical characterizations of slaves as shiftless, lazy, and conniving. His sermon concludes, "If you disobey your earthly master, you offend your heavenly Master." Jacobs leaves the meeting, "highly amused at brother Pikes' gospel teaching."[28] Her amusement is a result of the fact that she was literate and could read the Scriptures for herself and construct a "liberation theology" of her own. Jacobs, in fact, directly confronted her master on the issue of biblical interpretation on the occasion of one of his several attempts to make her his concubine. Despite having just joined the Episcopal church, her master again pleads with her to submit to his sexual advances, and she responds with a biblical defense of her refusal. With his voice "hoarse with rage," he exclaims, "'How dare you preach to me about your infernal Bible!'"[29] Jacobs closes the chapter by quoting the folk wisdom of the slave spirituals, "'Ole Satan's church is here below;/ Up to God's free church I hope to go.'" Here we hear the spirituals speaking with a double-voice, hoping to join God's free church in heaven and/or in the North.

"...both in this world and the next."

---

[28] Harriet Jacobs, *Incidents in the Life of a Slave Girl*, 69
[29] Ibid, 75.

THE BLACK CHURCH has placed, since its beginnings, an emphasis on scriptural knowledge and Bible reading and has had a different mission and history. Whereas the white church has emphasized an individualistic piety, what Charles Reagan Wilson calls the "finger sins" taught in Sunday school—"do not lie, do not cheat, do not covet your neighbor's possessions, do not lust even in your heart, do not drink alcoholic beverages"—, [30] the black church has helped its members, in the folk vernacular, to "make a way out of no way." The white southern church has tended to privilege what Faulkner, in *Light in August*, called a long list of "Thou Shalt Nots," and the black southern church has privileged narratives of deliverance to nurture its members. Granted, low-levels of black literacy in the early stages of the nineteenth-century black church prevented a widespread, true *reading* knowledge of the Bible. In fact, the Bible provided one of the greatest incentives for freedmen to learn to read so that they might develop their own biblical interpretations rather than the often-heard messages proclaiming their supposed inhumanity. Yet, African-American Christians, even those earliest worshipers who had the Bible read to them, continually demonstrated a thorough knowledge of the Bible and its stories, images, and tropes. Cain H. Felder attests to the reverent attention rendered to the Bible, the book which "has come to occupy a central place in the religion of the Black diaspora."[31] And as Lawrence Levine has demonstrated, you need look no further than the spirituals—with their "vivid biblical imagery, compelling sense of identification with the Children of Israel, and...tendency to dwell incessantly upon and to relive the

---

[30] Charles Reagan Wilson, "The Religious Culture: Distinctiveness and Social Change," 9

[31] Cain H. Felder, "The Bible, Re-Contextualization, and the Black Religious Experience," 155-56.

stories of the Old Testament"[32]—to find stirring evidence of this familiarity.

The black church's reverence for the Bible and its identification with select Bible stories can be traced to its earliest participation in evangelical Protestantism, particularly the Great Revival. It is no mere coincidence that the Baptists and Methodists led this region-wide revival and establishment of predominantly black churches.[33] From these revivals that swept across virtually the entire settled South, black churches "adopted wholesale the credal confessions and the governing and ritual formats of their white counterparts."[34] They also adopted "wholesale" what I call the Prime Imperative of Protestantism, that is, the mandate to personally study God's Word. Central to Protestantism's dissidence is a belief in the Priesthood of the Believer which constrains all believers to work out their salvation in fear and trembling, and this conversion is reinforced by personal readings of the Holy Scriptures. This examination of the Bible could be aided by a minister, but certainly required no mediation from a sanctioned ministerial representative or clergy member. The black church learned from white evangelical Christianity two important lessons in constructing a distinct African-American hermeneutic: 1) faith was to be interpreted in the light of the Bible and, 2) each person was free to interpret the Bible. While accepting the Bible as the central document of their religiosity, African-Americans chose to interpret it in their own fashion.[35]

Beginning with the earliest endeavors of the Society for the Propagation of the Gospel to proselytize slaves in 1701, African-Americans have struggled with their white brethren, attempting

---

[32] Lawrence Levine, *Black Culture and Black Consciousness: Afro-American Folk Thought from Slavery to Freedom*, 23.

[33] Hill, *South and the North in American Religion*, 24.

[34] C. Eric Lincoln, "Black Heritage in Religion of the South," 52-53.

[35] Vincent L. Wimbush, "The Bible and African-Americans: An Outline of an Interpretive History," 86, 89.

to wrest interpretation of God's Word away from a Christianity that neither affirmed nor validated their existence. As John B. Boles reminds us, sometimes that struggle for hermeneutical control occurred in biracial antebellum congregations: "Blacks heard the same sermons, took communion with whites, were buried in the same cemeteries, and participated in the church disciplinary procedures."[36] Despite these glimpses of equality, slaves who worshipped with whites were the objects of segregation (slaves were often forced to sit in balconies known as "nigger heaven") and condescension. As C. Eric Lincoln observes, slave-owning Christians' message to blacks was overwhelmingly a "gospel distorted by an insidious racism and compromised by self-conceit and economic self-interest."[37] Yet, inspired by leaders such as Richard Allen, who established the first recognized black church in America in 1794,[38] and from the preachers of the "Invisible Church," generations of African-American congregations have culled from this white-slanted Gospel a distinct, black, Christian religiosity.

African-Americans, beginning with the earliest antebellum slave preachers, adapted and transformed "the white man's message of subservient obedience into a confident awareness that things were not as they should be, or as they would be."[39] Black believers took the authority for this adaptation and transformation from their interpretations of the Bible as the iconic book of the Protestant heritage. By inheriting Protestantism's Prime Imperative, African-American congregations could justify their hermeneutical practices at least as strongly as their white brethren. The Bible gave the black church "the assurance of the ephemeral quality of the present situation and the glories and retribution to

---

36 Boles, "The Discovery of Southern Religious History," 520-21.

37 C. Eric Lincoln, "Development of Black Religion in America," 20.

38 Will B. Gravely, "The Rise of African Churches in America: (1786-1822): Re-Examining the Contexts," 302.

39 Lincoln, "Black Heritage in Religion of the South," 46.

come, both in this world and the next." Familiarity with the Bible provided paradigms — Daniel, David, Joshua, Jonah, Noah, and, especially, Moses — of deliverance in *this* world.[40]

The call to study God's Word certainly played a large role in the black church's rereading of the Bible given to it during its earliest days under white missionary supervision. As Theophus H. Smith demonstrates in *Conjuring Culture: Biblical Formations of Black America*, there is something deeply ingrained in African-American religiosity which revoices the Bible as a "magical formulary for...transforming history and culture."[41] Smith uses the metaphor of "conjuring," or African-American folk magic which can either harm or help, to explain how the Bible has been transformed in black religious experience into a numinous text of equality and deliverance. Smith ranges over African-American religion, literature, and folk culture, finding "ritually patterned behaviors and performative uses of language and symbols conveying a pharmacopeic or healing/harming intent and employing biblical figures."[42] Conjurors work with roots, charms, and spells, many of which come from the Bible, but Smith reads African-American leaders, such as Sojourner Truth,[43] Nat Turner and Denmark Vesey,[44] W. E. B. DuBois,[45] and Dr. Martin Luther King, Jr.[46] as cultural conjurors, that is, figures who have appropriated Biblical rhetoric and tropes in striving for deliverance in the here-and-now.

---

[40] Levine, *Black Culture and Black Consciousness: Afro-American Folk Thought from Slavery to Freedom*, 63, 50.

[41] Theophus H. Smith, *Conjuring Culture: Biblical Formations of Black America*, 3.

[42] Ibid, 6.

[43] Ibid, 167-76.

[44] Ibid, 159-60.

[45] Ibid, 131-33.

[46] Ibid, 209.

The white church was instrumental in legitimating, consolidating, and perpetuating its own "secular culture through the instrumentality of conservative Protestant Christianity."[47] On the other hand, the black church utilized paradigms such as the stories of Old Testament heroes to create a Christian theology and practice opposed to the biblically sanctioned, racist culture in which they lived. The dominant culture often justified its characterization of African-Americans as second-class citizens with biblical appeals. In contrast, as J. R. Washington, Jr. insists, the black church "is the quest for...freedom, justice, dignity, and equality of opportunity in this world because [its members] know it to be realized in the world to come."[48] The black church adopted the Bible as the revealed Word of God but invented a new hermeneutic for itself. From its beginnings in the "invisible institution" of the slave church, the black church viewed the Bible as a document of liberation, containing God's promise of delivery in the here-and-now.

The Southern Inheritance

As O'CONNOR, FAULKNER, Hurston, and Wright layer their work with biblical stories, symbols, images and myths, they reveal a key element of their inheritances as *Southerners*: the enduring cultural power of the Bible and the South's black and white religious traditions which surround it. Moreover, their intertextual practice shows one of the South's most abiding cultural conflicts: who may read the Bible and for what purpose? *Wise Blood, Light in August, Moses, Man of the Mountain*, and *Uncle Tom's Children* all participate in the South's struggles between whites and blacks over biblical interpretation. Each text wrestles with the question of

---

[47] Samuel S. Hill, "The South's Two Cultures," 29.

[48] Joseph R. Washington, Jr., "The Peculiar Peril and Promise of Black Folk Religion," 61.

whether the Bible is to aid in maintaining racial inequity, or to galvanize God's people into overturning Southern racial bigotry. Each work *evokes* the South's white and black biblical hermeneutical traditions, calling forth a powerful cultural resonance created by the region's reification of the Bible. Yet these texts' intertextual invocations of the Bible are never simplistic or naive. Their biblical intertexts reveal the paradox of intertextuality: to incorporate a fragment of text into another is often an act of homage, of respect paid to a distinguished predecessor, but intertextual citation is also a tool for critique. Intertextuality allows one to utilize that which is useful, powerful, or appropriate while at the same time adapting it, making it new through parody, elision, or some other type of subtle troping. What is borrowed from the Southern religious traditions—black and white—by each intertextual citation is a bit of the reified power accorded to biblical stories. In the South, the Bible tends to be granted an unsurpassable power for moral instruction. It is even venerated as physical object. Recognizing the authority rendered to *the* Book, O'Connor, Faulkner, Hurston, and Wright commandeer its central stories, characters, and tropes to voice their contributions to the South's debate over the Bible's uses.

O'Connor's work asserts her belief in the need for personal redemption through Christ to stop the grotesque violence she sees as perpetrated because of a willful distancing from God. Faulkner's intertextual practice demonstrates his wary ambivalence toward the white Southern religious community which believes itself to have experienced the regeneration advocated by evangelical Protestantism, yet which still commits acts of racial violence. Hurston's novel exemplifies Southern blacks' continual need to reinterpret the Bible to create a nurturing and sustaining community in the midst of this violently segregated and unregenerate region. However, Wright's intertextual practice calls for a new, politically invigorated reading of the black church's Bible as a necessary foundation to effectively activate a political African-American community. These four drastically different appeals to the Bible outline the distinctions between the white and black Southern religious traditions. In various ways, each work claims that a Southern revitalization will occur only after the region renews its biblical interpretations.

CHAPTER TWO:

"BACKWARDS TO BETHLEHEM": EVANGELICALISM IN FLANNERY O'CONNOR'S *WISE BLOOD*

I have found that violence is strangely capable of returning my characters to reality and preparing them to accept their moment of grace. Their heads are so hard that almost nothing else will do the work. This idea, that reality is something to which we must be returned at considerable cost, is one which is seldom understood by the casual reader.
— Flannery O'Connor

Think not that I am come to send peace on earth: I came not to send peace, but a sword.
— Matthew 10:34

FLANNERY O'CONNOR OFTEN spoke of the impact of her Christian views upon her art and claimed that her notion of reality was a supernatural one, a reality given meaning through her commitment to the Catholic church: "I am no disbeliever in spiritual purpose and no vague believer. I see from the standpoint of orthodox Christianity. This means that for me the meaning of life is centered in Redemption by Christ and what I see in the world I see in its relation to that."[49] This vigorous proclamation of Christian belief, which probably sounds so alien to most of *Wise Blood's* contemporary readers, distinguishes her intertextual use of the Bible from that of Faulkner, Hurston, and Wright. These other authors view the Bible as a contested site where each struggles with the white South's dominant religiosity, but O'Connor's *Wise Blood* actually endorses many tenets of that dominant religiosity. *Wise Blood* intertextually evokes the Bible to elicit a commitment of Christian faith from its readers. O'Connor seeks to modify her readers who, like her characters, she feels have become so hard-headed through unbelief that they too do not recognize the necessity of God's grace. While Faulkner, Hurston, and Wright invoke biblical stories to comment upon and critique prevailing Southern racial inequities, O'Connor replicates the way the white South traditionally used the Bible to deflect concern away from societal considerations toward matters of personal piety and salvation. What I am not attempting to do is to deny the strength of O'Connor's Catholic convictions; instead, I would like bring to light the common ground that she shared with the region's white Protestantism, namely, an emphasis upon spiritual regeneration above all else.

Her work seeks to change the wandering South, to confront it with the sword of Christian conviction so that her Southern readers will return to their region's (in her opinion) diminishing faith. An example in *Wise Blood* is Solace Layfield, murdered by Hazel Motes, who could be said to have been redeemed, saved by God's grace, as Haze runs him down with his Essex and then backs over the fallen prophet. Layfield dies with God's name upon his lips, asking for forgiveness of his sins.[50] Within *Wise Blood*,

---

[49] Flannery O'Connor, "Fiction Writer and His Country," 32.
[50] Flannery O'Connor, *Wise Blood*, 108.

violence is divorced from a social context and placed squarely within the theological realm; violence serves as a metaphor for Christian conversion. In a similar manner, O'Connor relentlessly pursues her readership, aggressively confronting them with the message that they are doomed if they persist in living without Christian redemption.

The violence her characters experience is the means by which O'Connor's evangelical message reaches her audience's ear. She felt the importance of her mission justified such measures, maintaining that you must "shout" or draw "large and startling figures" to reach the spiritually "hard of hearing" and "almost blind."[51] However, when shouting to the "hard of hearing," dissenting voices are often drowned out. To paraphrase the litany of many Southern Protestant preachers practicing baptism by immersion, O'Connor's fiction illustrates her characters' death to their old way of life and their rebirth into Christ to walk with Him. As Louise Gossett notes, "the crux of [O'Connor's] fiction is the human being's need to recognize the peril of damnation in which he lives."[52] Because of the confrontational tone of much of her non-fiction and the impassioned instructions she often gave on how she wanted her stories and novels to be read, many O'Connor critics have aligned themselves with her passionate advocacy of the Christian message and read her stories and novels only through the critical lens of evangelical Christianity. A partial list of the more memorable examples of such studies would include Sister Kathleen Feeley's *Flannery O'Connor: Voice of the Peacock*, John R. May's *The Pruning Word: The Parables of Flannery O'Connor*, Marshall Bruce Gentry's *Flannery O'Connor's Religion of the Grotesque*, Richard Giannone's *Flannery O'Connor and the Mystery of Love*, Robert H. Brinkmeyer's *The Art and Vision of Flannery O'Connor*, John F. Desmond's *Risen Sons: Flannery*

---

[51] O'Connor, "Fiction Writer and His Country" 33-34.
[52] Louise Y. Gossett, "Flannery O'Connor," 490.

O'Connor's Vision of History, and Harold Fickett's *Flannery O'Connor: Images of Grace*. Also, any number of essays taken from almost any issue of the *Flannery O'Connor Bulletin* demonstrate the same orthodoxy of critical approaches. For each of these critics, identifying with the author's faith is a prerequisite for correct reading of the fiction. In the introduction to *Flannery O'Connor: New Perspectives*, Sura P. Rath discusses the early reception of *Wise Blood*. Early critics were unaware of O'Connor's devout Christian beliefs and ascribed to her an unhealthy interest in seamy characters. It has only been after O'Connor inserted her infamous preface to the novel (which is reproduced in all subsequent editions) that critics have followed her lead in reproducing the text's theology. To take a recent example, Laura B. Kennelly's "Exhortation in *Wise Blood*: Rhetorical Theory as an Approach to Flannery O'Connor" encourages us to read the novel as an "exhortative" text. Of course, what we are exhorted to see is that "contemporary society face[s] a dangerous loss of spiritual awareness" and that "the saga of Hazel Motes and those around him [can] transmit a new way of seeing life..."[53] The rhetoric of the white South's salvation theology is nothing if not exhortative.

In the introduction to his recent anthology, *New Essays on Wise Blood*, Michael Kreyling announces that his particular collection "has been assembled not to reinforce the consensus on O'Connor's literary reputation, but to shake it a little out of complacent habits."[54] Kreyling convincingly argues that the result of these "complacent habits" has been "nearly five decades of repetitive affirmations of the theological message believed to inform O'Connor's work, reinforced by the tacit belief that her considerable suffering crowned her word with a special truth

---

[53] Laura B. Kennelly, "Exhortation in *Wise Blood*: Rhetorical Theory as an Approach to Flannery O'Connor,"166.

[54] Michael Kreyling, introduction to *New Essays on Wise Blood*, 2.

status."[55] Kreyling traces the general outline of O'Connor criticism, surveying attempts to read her works both "against" and "with" its theological grain. As a challenge, the essays in Kreyling's collection run counter to the majority of O'Connor criticism, in general, and *Wise Blood's* criticism, in particular. In this collection, *Wise Blood* is variously read as a critique of Cold War consumerism, the embodiment of Lacan's psychoanalytic theory of the gaze, and as an example of feminist resistance to male dominated culture and speech.

Each of the essays in the Kreyling volume tacitly confronts what Martha Stephens has labeled the "problem of assent"[56] in reading O'Connor's fiction. What if, unlike O'Connor herself, one does not read with the eyes of faith? Or, what if one does not read with O'Connor's faith, but with a faith more concerned with social justice? To take a smaller example before considering the novel *Wise Blood*, what is a critic such as Stephens or Andre Bleikasten, who raises many of the same questions, to make of a short story like "The River?" In this story, a young boy's parents—who could serve as the prototypes of worldly dissolution which so dismayed O'Connor—are too hung-over to attend to their son, so they leave him in the care of a good country woman who takes him to a "preaching and healing at the river."[57] There the preacher baptizes the boy, initiating him into his new life in the "Kingdom of Christ." The following day, while his parents are again hung-over, little Harry Ashfield slips out of their apartment and makes his way back to the river where he drowns trying to baptize himself again. As he goes under for the final time, he feels a "long gentle hand"[58] pulling him along the way toward a union with the saints. O'Connor explained her recurring tendency toward depicting

---

55 Ibid, 3.
56 Martha Stephens, *The Question of Flannery O'Connor*, 10.
57 Flannery O'Connor, *The Complete Stories*, 169.
58 Ibid, 174.

violent conversions by saying, "When I write a novel in which the central action is a baptism [referring to her second novel, *The Violent Bear It Away*], I am very well aware that for a majority of my readers, baptism is a meaningless rite, and so in my novel I have to see that this baptism carries enough awe and mystery to jar the reader into some kind of emotional recognition of its significance."[59] And the drowning of Harry Ashfield is quite jarring.

O'Connor anticipated most critics' recalcitrance to her sacramental vision and, concerning "The River" and Harry's ultimate fate, defended her work by embracing the white South's salvation-oriented religiosity: "[Harry] comes to a good end. He's saved from those nutty parents, a fate worse than death. He's been baptized and so he goes to his Maker; this is a good end."[60] The grief of the young boy's family, the pain of his death—neither of these factors is allowed to weaken the story's ending, nor are they acknowledged in O'Connor's insistence that her readers view this character's death only in the best possible terms. O'Connor's fiction invokes the Bible not in any openly revisionary sense—neither revising the white South's popular notions of the Bible nor that particular interpretive community itself—but as an authorization, an appeal, as if directly to the ultimate expression of God on Earth, His Holy Word.

O'Connor's evangelical intertextual appropriations from the Bible are very similar to one of the white South's strongest biblical interpreting strategies: the Bible's perceived evangelical thrust makes it more of a document of the relationship between God and humanity and less of a guidebook for the relationships between and among Southern whites and blacks. The title of O'Connor's second novel, *The Violent Bear It Away*, perfectly exemplifies a biblical intertext employed to spur her readers to Christian

---

[59] Flannery O'Connor, "Novelist and Believer," 162.
[60] *Conversations with Flannery O'Connor*, 58.

commitment. What could easily be interpreted as a call for political insurrection in the biblical text—"And from the days of John the Baptist until now the kingdom of heaven suffereth violence, and the violent take it by force"[61]—is read by the evangelical South (and most O'Connor critics) as a challenge to one's soul. Similarly, *Wise Blood*'s revoicings of the New Testament turn away social questions of racial injustice by focusing upon the efforts of true believers to claim the "kingdom of heaven." Thomas Schaub makes a similar point when he asserts that "throughout [her] fiction, it isn't too hard to see that...these violent conversions [of characters like Hazel Motes from *Wise Blood*] are meant to operate as much against the liberal reader as against the central character."[62] Schaub's *American Fiction in the Cold War* does a remarkable job of placing O'Connor's fiction within the context of Cold War liberalism and its rhetoric, arguing that "the premises of O'Connor's work were remarkably consistent with those of the very audience she imagined withering under her attack."[63] The common premises that Schaub detects between her fiction and the discourse of modern American liberalism are a belief in human imperfection, the presence of evil, and a "necessity to recognize the limitations of human control and aspiration."[64] Despite this common ground, O'Connor often saw herself as being at odds with these "liberal readers," whom she often labeled "innerlekchuls" in her correspondence, and she was hesitant of making tactical alliances with those who did not share her uncompromising Christian faith.

As she appropriates biblical material, O'Connor's identification and shared sympathies with Southern Protestantism influence her intertextual project, giving her a different agenda from the rest of

---

[61] Matthew 11:12.
[62] Thomas Schaub, *American Fiction in the Cold War*, 123.
[63] Ibid, 125.
[64] Ibid, 124.

the authors in this study. For example, William Faulkner's intertextual use of the Bible in *Light in August* assails the white Southern Protestantism that views the Scriptures as a divinely sanctioned statement of white superiority. Through his depiction of Yoknapatawpha County's fear and hatred of Joe Christmas, he exposes the white community's use of the Bible to authorize Christmas's eventual lynching. Hurston's *Moses, Man of the Mountain* creates an alternative African-American world apart from the oppressive white South, and Wright's Dan Taylor and Aunt Sue from *Uncle Tom's Children* employ a distinctly black religiosity as a foundation for the fight against Jim Crow. Both *Moses, Man of the Mountain,* and *Uncle Tom's Children* utilize the black church's theological legacies to inform their respective intertextual practices. Whereas Hurston and Wright adopt elements from the black church's struggle against an oppressive society, and Faulkner reveals the racism of a small but vocal biblical interpretive community, O'Connor's intertextual practice replicates the white church's silence over unjust racial practices that arose from a militant emphasis upon personal salvation and redemption.

Kreyling is right in his insistence that the critical orthodoxy surrounding O'Connor has resulted in an "orthodox line [that] is narrow, deep, and resistant to revision."[65] And his anthology, along with Jon Lance Bacon's *Flannery O'Connor and Cold War Culture,* does much to redirect the attention focused on *Wise Blood* and the rest of O'Connor's fiction. However, that is not to denigrate the theologically informed investigations which have already revealed great insights into her work or to suggest that there is nothing else to be gained from such investigations. Indeed, in one sense, this chapter is but another religiously-oriented investigation of *Wise Blood,* but with two important differences: first, I want to point to the shared concerns of *Wise*

---

[65] Kreyling, introduction to *New Essays on Wise Blood,* 7.

Blood and the dominant religiosity of the white South's silence over racial matters; and, secondly, I want to place O'Connor's evangelical fervor in dialogue with other biblically shaped texts, which reflect the variety of the Southern religious experience.

This salvational emphasis of the white South, though diminished, still characterizes the region known as the Bible Belt. O'Connor stresses that the South is the last remaining region of America where Sam Jones's[66] grandma would read "the Bible thirty-seven times on her knees," and it is "made up of the descendants of old ladies like her. You don't shake off their influence in even several generations."[67] What white Southerners have inherited but not "shaken off" from figures such as Grandmother Jones is a common medium of expression, a shared set of images, allusions, stories, and tropes which provides them with a common vocabulary emphasizing the soul's need for salvation. Reading the Bible in the South is the pursuit of literate individuals from all classes, from the educated upper classes to the poorest dirt farmers.[68] As a devoted reader and student of the Scriptures herself, O'Connor uses the Bible as her primary "instrument to plumb Christian meaning."[69] O'Connor uses biblical intertexts to invest her characters' struggles with a religious urgency and ground them in the supernatural reality she believed in so strongly herself.

Because of her adamant Catholicism, O'Connor might seem an outsider among a grouping of Southern writers that includes

---

[66] Samuel Porter Jones (1846-1906) was one of America's most popular evangelical preachers in the late nineteenth and very early twentieth centuries He swore at his father's deathbed to forsake alcohol and his profligate lifestyle, accepted Christianity shortly afterward and preached his first sermon within a week after his conversion (Henry Warner Bowden, "Samuel Porter Jones," 367).

[67] O'Connor, "Catholic Novelist in the Protestant South" 201-202.

[68] Ibid, 203.

[69] Ibid, 209.

William Faulkner, Zora Neale Hurston, and Richard Wright. As Southern historians, and Southern historians of religion in particular, have long known, the overwhelmingly Protestant South, outside of a few areas, has not been very tolerant or accepting of Catholics. Louis D. Rubin was given perhaps only to slight exaggeration in his characterization of many Southern Protestants of the 1950s and 1960s when he described them as believing that "the Pope of Rome is a minion of Satan, and a Catholic priest a mysterious and dangerous man."[70] An earlier generation's animosity toward and blaming of Catholics for the ills of the region and the nation can be found in an article in the *Memphis Commercial Appeal* from 1928 which claimed that "three of our presidents have been assassinated, and it is understood that every one of them fell at the hands of Catholics. I have never heard a statement to the contrary."[71] However, as a Southerner, O'Connor received what Rubin calls a "double heritage,"[72] a Catholic doctrinal orthodoxy along with a knowledge of and affinity for the region's evangelical fundamentalism. As to the latter component of her amalgamated theological heritage, O'Connor discusses these submerged or "underground affinities" in her essay, "The Catholic Novelist in the Protestant South." She defines the Protestant South as the last region of America where Christianity and Bible reading have not been demoted to a "department of sociology…or personality development," either of which would have appalled O'Connor. She claims that in the South, at least, the supernatural is not an embarrassment. Because of her concern with saving souls and her commitment to personal Bible study, O'Connor proclaims a religious "kinship" with

---

[70] Louis D. Rubin, "Flannery O'Connor and the Bible Belt," 50.

[71] Quoted in Kenneth K Bailey, *Southern White Protestantism in the Twentieth Century*, 104.

[72] Rubin, "Flannery O'Connor and the Bible Belt," 74.

Protestant "backwoods prophets and shouting fundamentalists."[73] As she explained elsewhere, "in the South the general conception of man is still, in the main, theological."[74]

More specifically, O'Connor's kinship with her Protestant neighbors results from a shared belief in the "divinity of Christ,...the Redemptive Power, [and] the physical resurrection."[75] O'Connor maintained that the differences she had with Southern Protestants were "on the nature of the Church, not on the nature of God or our obligation to Him."[76] O'Connor wrote to the novelist John Hawkes that she accepted "the same fundamental doctrines of sin and redemption and judgement"[77] as her Southern Protestant fellow-believers. Despite differences of denominational loyalty, a white Southern "Child of God" — whether Sam Jones or Flannery O'Connor — would know his or her spiritual brothers and sisters because he or she would recognize a similar concern with salvation.

Samuel S. Hill characterizes the emphasis placed upon personal salvation by the white South as "verticalist."[78] This term emphasizes the dominant relationship of the white South's theology, a relationship plotted along a vertical axis between a morally requiring God and sinful humans. Conversion, or in the white church's vocabulary, "getting right with God," is necessary to establish this vertical bond. Southern social ills such as child labor, sharecropping, illiteracy, and race relations received little attention from the region's religion because the white church

---

[73] Flannery O'Connor, "Catholic Novelist in the Protestant South," 207.

[74] Flannery O'Connor, "Southern Fiction," 44.

[75] Rubin, "Flannery O'Connor and the Bible Belt," 69 See Robert Brinkmeyer's *The Art and Vision of Flannery O'Connor* for another insightful discussion of the common spiritual concerns O'Connor shared with her Protestant neighbors.

[76] O'Connor, "Catholic Novelist in the Protestant South," 202.

[77] Flannery O'Connor, *The Habit of Being*, 350.

[78] Samuel S. Hill, *Southern Churches in Crisis*, 92.

emphasized "the temporary nature of this world as a place whose evils must be endured."[79] O'Connor's own verticalist disposition is apparent in *Mystery and Manners* when she proclaims her readers' need to realize their "dependence on the grace of God [for salvation], and a knowledge that evil is not simply a problem to be solved, but a mystery to be endured."[80] Much like the Southern white church, whose religion is "dominantly a conservative or reinforcing agent for the traditional values held by white Southern society,"[81] O'Connor's focus on the soul's condition de-emphasizes the region's social concerns.

The "story" necessary for constructing O'Connor's fiction is the story of individual sinners' redemption that white Southern Protestants stress in their evangelical, salvation-oriented interpre-tations of the Bible. In *Wise Blood*, O'Connor utilizes her familiarity with the Bible and relies upon a similar, although perhaps lesser, knowledge in her Southern readership. As she says elsewhere: "Abstractions, formulas, laws will not serve here. We have to have stories in our background. It takes a story to make a story. It takes a story of mythic dimensions, one that belongs to everybody, one in which everybody is able to recognize the hand of God and its descent. In the Protestant South, the Scriptures fill this role."[82] O'Connor's fiction then is to lead readers back to its narrative source—the Bible. This reading of the Bible as a single, sustained narrative which relates the Christian story of Christ's redemption is common to Protestantism. For example, theologian Carl Ficken's *God's Story and Modern Literature* succinctly summarizes this hermeneutical principle: "The Christian's life and faith are shaped within a community that exists because of the great *story* of God's freeing and sustaining love. The Bible tells that story; the

---

79 Samuel S. Hill, "The South's Two Cultures," 41.
80 O'Connor, "Catholic Novelist in the Protestant South," 209.
81 Hill, "The South's Two Cultures," 36.
82 O'Connor, "Catholic Novelist in the Protestant South," 202.

church has repeated it, lived it, been nourished by it for centuries. We are a people who know how to read a story and how to tell one."[83] Upon (re)turning to the Bible, readers will find what the white South's Protestant tradition finds in its "infallible Bible,... especially the King James version of it"[84]: the salvation story. In white Southern religiosity, the Bible provides insight into the state of one's soul—will you stand before a demanding God as an unregenerate sinner, or as a redeemed believer? White Southern ministers and their congregations often deflected issues of race relations because they did not conceive of the region's "race problem" as a matter of individual morality.

For O'Connor, the relationship between her fiction and the Bible is an anagogical one, revealing the link between the known world and the supernatural reality embodied in Christ's incarnation, His redemptive death, and His resurrection. O'Connor often referred to the anagogical element present in what she considered good fiction: "The kind of vision the fiction writer needs to have, or to develop, in order to increase the meaning of his story is called anagogical vision, and that is the kind of vision that is able to see different levels of reality in one image or one situation." Within her own work, she strove to invest her writing with an "anagogical vision" in an effort to reveal "the Divine life and our participation in it."[85] *Wise Blood's* biblical intertextuality, the novel's prime anagogical manifestation, is "verticalist" in much the same way that O'Connor's theology is verticalist; the novel invokes the Bible to insist upon personal salvation dispensed by a morally demanding God to whom everyone will one day be accountable. O'Connor appropriates biblical stories, figures, characters, and tropes so that her work might echo with the same urgent redemptive message she finds so prevalent in the

---

83 Carl Ficken, *God's Story and Modern Literature*, ix-x.
84 Edgar T. Thompson, "God and the Southern Plantation System," 61.
85 Flannery O'Connor, "The Nature and Aim of Fiction," 72.

Scriptures. Her own reading of the Bible and her intertextual appropriations mediate between her fiction and the supernatural realm it seeks to engage. O'Connor invokes the WORD into her words, investing *Wise Blood* with seemingly timeless and universal qualities, but her intertextual revoicings actually reflect the reading practices of a specific time and place. *Wise Blood's* intertexts reflect the white South's obsession with individual sin and salvation.

This sin/salvation fixation is encapsulated in *Wise Blood's* twin characters of unbelief and belief, Enoch Emery and Hazel Motes, respectively, whose exploits demonstrate O'Connor's fervent belief in the necessity of spiritual rebirth. In O'Connor's fiction, each individual must choose Christ, as does Haze, or the world, as does Enoch. As Robert Brinkmeyer has noted, a fundamentalist, evangelical theology, which is embodied in Haze's mother and grandfather, underpins the novel.[86] "Every fourth Saturday," Hazel's grandfather drove "into Eastrod as if he were just in time to save them all from Hell, and he was shouting before he had the car door open."[87] And the message the old man delivered was extremely simple — all listeners must surrender to the "soul-hungry" Jesus or they will face the Hell from which Jesus was so desperate to save them. There are no fine theological points or room for discussion — one must choose redemption or damnation, Jesus or the world.

As they move through Taulkinham,[88] Enoch and Haze are anagogically linked to the Bible in two ways: their names render

---

[86] Brinkmeyer, *The Art and Vision of Flannery O'Connor*, 105.

[87] Ibid, 10.

[88] Several critics have discussed the symbolic function of Taulkinham in relation to some of the more decadent cities of the Bible See Thomas Lorch, "Flannery O'Connor: Christian Allegorist," for a reading of *Wise Blood* which examines O'Connor's debt to Christian allegorists, such as Bunyan, and which reads Taulkinham as a contemporary version of Vanity Fair; Horton Davies, "Anagogical Signals in O'Connor's Fiction,"

moral pronouncements on life's vacuity outside of Christ, and their actions reveal their desperate longing for some supernatural significance in their lives. Emily Archer concludes that O'Connor's "consistent attention to meaningful, unarbitrary character naming should...be perceived as an *anagogical* signal, a clue that names can somehow 'make contact with mystery'"[89] (emphasis added). For example, Enoch Emery is an intertextual revoicing of two different Enoch's from the early chapters of Genesis.[90] The first is the son of Cain, born after his father was cursed for killing Abel.[91] In his wanderings, Cain founded a city which he named after his first born son. The white South's religiosity interprets this Enoch (Cain's son) as a figure for sinful man. Therefore, Enoch Emery's name links him to this first Enoch's Old Testament story; Enoch Emery is the "son" of the Bible's first example of willfulness and distance from God after the Fall. The familial connection between O'Connor's character and the Old Testament Cain is further revealed when Enoch mentions his daddy's scar to Haze. Like his intertextual biblical predecessor, Enoch Emery is a man living under a system of rituals, outside of the Grace of Christ, completely clueless about Jesus' redemptive mission. Despite Enoch Emery's boast that he knows a "whole heap about Jesus,"[92]

---

for a catalogue of recurring religious symbols in the depiction of *Wise Blood*'s apostate Southern city; and Sallie McFague, "The Parabolic in Faulkner, O'Connor, and Percy," in which she finds that, like the Gospel parables of Christ, O'Connor's fiction is rooted in the everyday world while revealing a supernatural reality. See also Marshall Bruce Gentry's *Flannery O'Connor's Religion of the Grotesque*, particularly 123-24, for an insightful discussion of the absent and/or twisted theologies of Taulkinham's citizens.

[89] Emily Archer, "'Stalking Joy': Flannery O'Connor's Accurate Naming," 22.

[90] James L. Green, "Enoch Emery and His Biblical Namesakes in *Wise Blood*," 418.

[91] Genesis 4:17.

[92] *Wise Blood*, 26.

he fruitlessly seeks to fulfill his spiritual impulses through a series of rituals in the park, such as his viewing of the shrunken mummy,[93] without an evangelical faith in Christian redemption. These rituals display Enoch's religious nature, but in O'Connor's redemption-oriented vocabulary, he is only "Christ-haunted" and never "Christ-centered." Enoch symbolizes for O'Connor the component within humanity "that demands the redemptive act,"[94] yet he is unable to convert the factual knowledge of Jesus he acquired at the Rodemill Boys Bible Academy into a practicing Christian faith. For O'Connor, faith can never be just a matter of facts or biographical knowledge about the life of Jesus.

Enoch Emery's intertextual relationship with the second Enoch of Genesis is ironic. This second Old Testament Enoch was the child of Adam and Eve's third son, Seth. This Enoch was a righteous man and a Hebrew patriarch from whose descendants Noah would eventually be born. Genesis 5:24 describes this Enoch walking with God, avoiding death, and being taken directly into communion with God: "...and he *was* not; for God took him." Unlike every other patriarch listed in the genealogy between Adam and Noah, the length of Enoch's life is never given. In the New Testament, the writer of Hebrews revoices Enoch's story to demonstrate the rewards of godly living: "By faith Enoch was translated that he should not see death; and was not found, because God had translated him: for before his translation he had this testimony, that he pleased God."[95]

In an ironic retelling of this biblical story, O'Connor also "translates" her Enoch from what the white South's theology would consider a spiritually vacuous human being into an animal,

---

[93] Harold Fickett also argues that Enoch's religious desires are revealed through the rituals he constantly performs and even goes so far as to liken them to a type of liturgy (Harold Fickett, *Flannery O'Connor: Images of Grace*, 42-43).

[94] O'Connor, "Southern Fiction," 48.

[95] Hebrews 11:5.

both of whom lack the ability to connect with God. All of Enoch's innate religious desires are twisted by Taulkinham's consumerism. For instance, O'Connor's Enoch's greatest goal is to be "THE young man of the future, like the ones in the insurance ads."[96] In the theological framework of the white South, the logical conclusion of Enoch's quest to fulfill his religion of self-advancement is when he becomes an animal, assuming the form of a gorilla and being translated into an *it*.[97] As Enoch dresses himself in the gorilla-suit, O'Connor shifts from the human pronoun "he" to the inhuman pronoun "it":

> In the uncertain light, one of his lean white legs could be seen to disappear and then the other, one arm and then the other: a black heavier shaggier figure replaced his. For an instant, it had two heads, one light and one dark, but after a second, it pulled the dark back head over the other and corrected this. It busied itself with certain hidden fastenings and what appeared to be minor adjustments of its hide.[98]

After worshipping the shriveled mummy, the unregenerate god of pop psychology and profit-motive theology, Enoch Emery's deity rewards him, and "no gorilla in existence, whether in the jungles of Africa or California, or in New York City in the finest apartment in the world, was happier at that moment than this one."[99]

---

[96] *Wise Blood*, 98 See Jon Lance Bacon's essay, "A Fondness for Supermarkets: *Wise Blood* and Consumer Culture," and his book-length study, *Flannery O'Connor and Cold War Culture*, for investigations of *Wise Blood* as critique of rampant American consumerism.

[97] See William Allen's "The Cage of Matter: The World as Zoo in Flannery O'Connor's *Wise Blood*" for a discussion of Enoch's "translation" into the gorilla Allen sees this change as prefigured in Enoch's fascination with the zoo animals and as a reward for the religious offices performed at the zoo.

[98] *Wise Blood*, 101.

[99] Ibid, 102.

In an example of a critic replicating *Wise Blood's* verticalist theology, Richard Giannone appropriates O'Connor's and the white South's rhetoric of Christian salvation when he writes of this scene, "the Enoch of Genesis may have been translated to heaven..., but the gorilla on the rock is humanity shorn of glory."[100] But the translation of Enoch Emery from man to gorilla reveals *Wise Blood's* deferral to prevailing Southern opinions on race. The South's racist images of blacks as sub-human beasts lurk just beneath the surface of this scene. By the end of the transformation, Enoch is a black, shaggy brute completely ruled by base or "animal" desires. In attempting to demonstrate that all humans urgently need a regenerative encounter with Christ, O'Connor creates a portrait precariously close to the white South's stereotypical menacing black male. Enoch's metaphorical transformation sounds suspiciously close to the core of Gavin Stevens' speech about Joe Christmas's "warring" white and black blood from *Light in August*: both men succumb to inherent weaknesses. Both Hazel and Joe Christmas wage a losing fight against their "darker" natures before completely submitting to their evil inheritances. O'Connor's insistence that her fiction be interpreted using anagogical principles deflects attention away from possible racial considerations. For O'Connor and the evangelical white South, racial injustice is not a matter of individual piety but simply a worldly injustice to be endured.

While O'Connor links Enoch Emery to the Old Testament, demonstrating the consequences of life without Jesus, Hazel Motes is intertextually linked primarily to the New Testament. His name invokes the pervasive New Testament imagery of blindness because first Haze is blind to God's summons, and then he so completely submits to God that he blinds himself so that he will not be distracted from his newly acquired spiritual vision. Hazel Motes' name comes from Jesus' admonition in Matthew 7:3-5:

---

[100] Richard Giannone, *Flannery O'Connor and the Mystery of Love*, 25.

"And why beholdest thou the mote that is in thy brother's eye, but considerest not the beam that is in thine own eye? Or how wilt thou say to thy brother, Let me pull out the mote out of thine eye; and, behold, a beam is in thine own eye? Thou hypocrite, first cast out the beam out of thine own eye; and then shalt thou see clearly to cast out the mote out of thy brother's eye." In *Wise Blood's* theological framework, the young man from Eastrod is blind to God's call because of the obfuscating "haze" of his apostasy and the log-sized "mote" of personal pride in his own eye, i.e., thinking he has not sinned and does not need salvation. Haze's metaphorical and literal blindness evoke a large network of New Testament images all connected by the white South to proper seeing, that is, the ability to distinguish Jesus' teachings and how one is to follow them. For instance, Christ proclaims that "the light of the body is the eye," and if it is filled with light, "then thy whole body shall be filled with light."[101] In O'Connor's revoicing of this New Testament trope, before his conversion when he acquired his spiritual sight and lost his physical sight, Haze was guilty of having eyes, yet having no sight.[102]

As spiritually exhortative as O'Connor intends their names to be, Enoch Emery and Hazel Motes most dramatically reveal O'Connor's project of evangelical biblical intertextuality through their actions. For the reader initiated into the white South's redemption-oriented theology, nearly everything they do points toward the futility of life without God's grace while encouraging readers to return to or establish relationships with Christ. For example, the anagogical significance of Enoch's pursuit of the "new jesus," which he believes to have found in the shriveled mummy, clearly reveals O'Connor's scorn for false idols. O'Connor uses a key word from her religious vocabulary to describe the mummy and its significance to Enoch: "It was a

---

[101] Matthew 6:23
[102] Mark 8:18

mystery, although it was right there in a glass case for everybody to see and there was a typewritten card over it telling all about it. But there was something the card couldn't say..."[103] (emphasis added). What this shriveled little man cannot communicate to Enoch is some sense of the divine Mystery (as O'Connor usually designated it) of God's redemptive involvement in and concern for individuals.

O'Connor's disdain for such frail idols is revealed in her manipulation of biblical intertexts surrounding Enoch's veneration of the mummy and its rewards. Compelled by his vague spiritual yearnings, Enoch begins to clean his rented room for the arrival of his sacred visitor. The object receiving the most attention, since it will be the future home of his god, is a washstand which was "built in three parts and stood on bird legs six inches high.... The lowest part was a *tabernacle-like cabinet which was meant to contain a slop-jar*"[104] (emphasis added). He paints the inside of his tabernacle with gilt paint and places the mummy inside of what O'Connor, in an obvious allusion to the Hebrew Ark of the Covenant, calls an "ark."[105] Like a chief priest from the Old Testament, Enoch now waits for directions from his god, whose relics are to be housed in a completely secular version of the Ark of the Covenant inside the holy of holies of Enoch's room. For O'Connor, the mummy is no more spiritually enlightening than the human excrement that used to fill the slop-jar the washstand was designed to hold. The result of Enoch's willful pursuit of this new jesus is already apparent: he spiritually de-evolves from a human being and is translated from a person into an "it."

O'Connor once described Enoch as a "moron and chiefly a comic character."[106] O'Connor is able to laugh the laugh of the

---

103 *Wise Blood*, 41.
104 Ibid, 67.
105 Ibid, 89.
106 Flannery O'Connor, "On Her Own Work," 116.

justified because of her firm religious faith. If readers find humor in Enoch's exploits, there is little to laugh at in the grim spectacle of Haze working out his salvation "in fear and trembling" and numerous mortifications of the flesh. Not only does Haze blind himself in his quest for redemption, but in the last days of his life, he also wraps barbed wire around his chest and fills his shoes with pebbles and broken glass. To understand Haze's struggle against unbelief, one must understand the Motes family's religious legacy. Haze received some of his earliest teaching about Christ from the frightening figure of his grandfather, "a waspish old man who had ridden over three counties with Jesus hidden in his head like a stinger."[107] The grandfather spoke of a relentless, frightening, "soul-hungry" Jesus who would chase sinners "over the waters of sin," and despite any obstacle, He "would have them in the end."[108] As O'Connor herself claimed, the only thing that Hazel retained from this frightening exposure to his grandfather's evangelical tirades was "a sense of sin.... This sense of sin is the only key he has to finding a sanctuary and he begins unconsciously to search for God *through* sin" (emphasis added).[109] This quest for redemption, regardless of where it might lead, is the common ground that forms the religious kinship with the white South's evangelical Protestantism, which O'Connor acknowledged in her "underground affinities" with "back-woods prophets" and "shouting fundamentalists." By the novel's conclusion, Hazel does

---

[107] *Wise Blood*, 9.

[108] Ibid, 10.

[109] Quoted in Fickett, *Flannery O'Connor: Images of Grace*, 39 In this passage, Fickett is quoting from an unpublished letter of O'Connor's written as a summary of *Wise Blood* for potential publishers. She wrote this letter before *Wise Blood* was accepted for publication by Robert Giroux, who would eventually publish all of her work, and after John Selby had released her from a contract given to her based upon the merit of her early stories and her M.F.A. thesis.

not seem to even be living in this world, much less showing any concern for its injustices.

O'Connor dramatizes Haze's willful rebellion and flight—both in terms of theology and geography—from his calling from God in the opening and closing scenes of chapter 7. Just as God directed Moses and the Israelite nation out of Egyptian bondage with a cloud to direct them by day, He also seeks to lead Hazel with a cloud, one reminiscent of an Old Testament patriarch: "The sky was just a little lighter blue than [Hazel's] suit, clear and even, with only one cloud in it, a large blinding white one with curls and a beard."[110] Hazel, however, is too busy trying to seduce Sabbath Hawkes (who is busy trying to seduce Hazel) to take notice of God's attempts at spiritual guidance. By the end of the chapter, the cloud-image of an Old Testament, patriarchal figure has given way to "a bird with long thin wings and was disappearing in the opposite direction."[111] O'Connor's text seems eager to bestow upon Hazel an anointing similar to Christ's when the Holy Spirit descended upon Him in the form of a dove.[112] The distance between Haze's theology and that of the evangelical South—which reads this New Testament story as the starting point of Christ's redemptive mission—is revealed in the simple act of Hazel driving "in the opposite direction" of this heavenly sign. Despite their nearly constant grumbling against Jehovah and the insurrections they mount against Moses, even Hurston's recalcitrant Hebrews from *Moses, Man of the Mountain* are more spiritually attuned to God's signs than Hazel.

The clouds in the countryside are not the only signs O'Connor has placed in Hazel's path that he fails to read, signs which become increasingly obvious to the reader attuned to her evangelical project. Haze commits the sin of pride when he repeatedly

---

[110] *Wise Blood*, 60.

[111] Ibid, 65.

[112] Matthew 3:16; Mark 1:10; Luke 3:22; John 1:32.

claims not to need Christ's intervention for salvation, as he tells the waitress at the zoo's restaurant, "I AM clean." So, with the log-sized mote of pride in his own eye, Haze cannot read such subtle signs as the clouds. Hazel is so blind to the efforts of the "soul-hungry Jesus" that before his conversion he also fails to interpret correctly the most obvious signs the "wild ragged figure"[113] of the relentless Jesus places before him. These are literally the road-side signs whose fundamentalist urgency demands that Haze abandon his sinful ways. On a trip out of the city, Haze sees a gray boulder beside the road. "White letters on the boulder said, WOE TO THE BLASPHEMER AND WHOREMONGER! WILL HELL SWAL-LOW YOU UP?"[114] Haze spends several minutes pondering the sign's question, one of special significance for Hazel, considering his involvement in the Church Without Christ and with Leora Watts, and for O'Connor's apostate readership whom he represents within *Wise Blood's* narrative world. Here O'Connor reveals her affinity with the evangelical white South, the large capital letters shouting to the spiritually deaf. Haze especially studies "the two words at the bottom of the sign. They said in smaller letters, 'Jesus Saves.'" Haze reacts with anger and declares, "I don't believe in anything."[115] The Church Without Christ says that there are no longer signs from God, if there ever were any, so Haze returns to Taulkinham unaware that Christ is preparing an unmistakable message for the recalcitrant young man from Eastrod. Or, is it O'Connor preparing an unmistakable message for us as readers?

O'Connor again reflects the conversion-oriented theology of the white South as she depicts three events which facilitate Hazel's eventual confrontation with an otherworldly Jesus: Hazel destroys the dust-filled new jesus; he kills the false prophet, Solace

---

[113] *Wise Blood*, 10.
[114] Ibid, 38.
[115] Ibid, 39.

Layfield; and the patrolman pushes his car over the embankment. In the first of these events, Enoch thinks he is rendering a great service to his deity by uniting the mummy with Hazel whom he supposes to be a great prophet of his secular god, a sort of John the Baptist whose lone voice in the wilderness of Taulkinham is preparing the way for this physical, unregenerate god. Yet what causes Hazel to reject this new jesus is what O'Connor once called his own type of "Wise Blood,"[116] a blood, unlike Enoch's, that intuitively recognizes that the shriveled mummy is not what he has been pursuing. Having never been anything more than "all man" and possessing no blood to spare for humanity's redemption, this new jesus serves no spiritually redemptive purpose for O'Connor. Hazel recognizes this when his vision is made hyperacute by putting on his mother's Bible-reading glasses and viewing the tableau of Sabbath cradling the shrunken mummy, an intertextual parody of the Catholic iconography of Madonna and Holy Child: she holds the shriveled little corpse "in the crook of her arm,...fitted exactly into the hollow of her shoulder."[117] Hazel responds to this blasphemous mother and child with great violence — he throws the new jesus against a wall, "and the trash inside sprayed out like dust."[118] He then throws the skin out the back door into the rain. Harold Fickett, in a passage whose rhetoric is virtually indistinguishable from O'Connor's, or the white South's dominant religiosity, concludes that "Haze...recognizes that he has indeed been presented with a new jesus — a jesus shrunken to the size to which Hazel's unbelief would tailor him; a jesus that is a continuing sign of our mortality, that lives on in a mummified eternity only to proclaim the impossibility of resurrection."[119] O'Connor says much the same

---

[116] O'Connor, *The Habit of Being*, 350.
[117] *Wise Blood*, 94-95.
[118] Ibid, 96.
[119] Fickett, *Flannery O'Connor: Images of Grace*, 43.

thing in a letter to "A"[120] dated 23 July 1960: "That Haze rejects the mummy suggests everything. What he has been looking for with body and soul throughout the book is suddenly presented to him and he sees it has to be rejected, he sees it ain't really what he's been looking for."[121] Hazel's momentary insight does not accomplish his redemption; rather, it is merely a step in clearing away the log-sized mote of personal pride that prevents him from recognizing his need for a redemptive encounter with Jesus.

The second event preparing Hazel for conversion—paradoxical as it may sound—is his killing of his narrative twin, Solace Layfield. Layfield is Hazel's textual double: when Hoover Shoats realizes that Hazel will not compromise his Church Without Christ for monetary gain, he simply hires a Hazel look-alike to help him work his scam. Hazel moves toward conversion when he strips away his double's pious costume.

> [Layfield] began to run in earnest. He tore off his shirt and unbuckled his belt and ran out of the trousers. He began grabbing for his feet as if he would take off his shoes too, but before he could get at them, the Essex knocked him flat and ran over him. Haze drove about twenty feet and stopped the car and then began to back it. He backed it over the body and then stopped and got out.[122]

Earlier, a woman in the crowd asked Hazel if he and Shoats's "True Prophet" were twins, and Hazel foreshadows Layfield's impending murder when he replies, "If you don't hunt it down

---

120 "A" is the designation given by Sally Fitzgerald in her editing of O'Connor's correspondence to a woman who first wrote to O'Connor in 1955 "A" wished to remain anonymous in O'Connor's collected letters. She and O'Connor wrote to each other from 1955 until O'Connor's death in 1964.

121 O'Connor, *The Habit of Being*, 404.

122 *Wise Blood*, 105.

and kill it, it'll hunt you down, and kill you."[123] This comment does not so much reveal Hazel's murderous tendencies as it does his realization, at least on what O'Connor considered his intuitive or "blood" level, that he must rid his own self of its disbelieving elements. Put another way, within the anagogical interpretive mode favored by *Wise Blood* and the Southern white church, Hazel's violence is interpreted not so much a murder of Layfield as it is a violent exorcism of his own sinful elements that obstruct his view of the redeeming Christ. Anagogy displaces the moral concerns regarding violence in the here and now. In the terms of O'Connor's universe, Hazel functions as Layfield's instrument of grace because, as the consumptive false prophet lies beneath the Essex, he confesses his sinful nature before Jesus and dies asking for His forgiveness: "'Jesus hep me,' the man wheezed."[124]

The final step of Hazel's preparation for conversion is when the patrolman destroys Hazel's car. Though Haze claims that not even a lightning bolt could stop his Essex, he does not reckon on the mysterious patrolman who polices the outer limits of Haze's apostasy and prohibits him from getting too far in his attempts to outrun God. This point is reinforced by another road sign that Hazel deliberately tries not to read—"Jesus Died for YOU"[125]—just moments before the policeman pulls him over. The officer pushes his car over an embankment, destroying his vehicle and his ability to run from God. "Haze stood for a few minutes, looking over at the scene. His face seemed to reflect the entire distance across the clearing and on beyond, the entire distance

---

123 Ibid, 85.

124 Ibid, 105. This scene from *Wise Blood* is particularly reminiscent of several O'Connor short stories where murder and mayhem serve as the agents of God's grace, bringing the victims to some saving knowledge of Christ. The Misfit, from "A Good Man is Hard to Find," is probably the best known and most often studied example of this tendency in O'Connor's work.

125 Ibid, 106.

that extended from his eyes to the blank gray sky that went on, depth after depth, into space. His knees bent under him and he sat down on the edge of the embankment with his feet hanging over."[126] Hazel has now completed his third prepatory experience necessary for receiving Jesus' mysterious redemptive grace.

This scene secures the intertextual bond between Hazel and Paul: both men violently experience God's grace as they travel isolated country roads to preach their individual messages against the Gospel. Immediately following his encounter with the patrolman, Haze rushes back to the city to blind himself with the mixture of quicklime and water. The blindness of Saul and Hazel is the bridge between their old selves and their new ones. Saul's blindness, the scales covering his eyes, is God's chastening tool. After his rebirth as the apostle Paul, he continually suffered from a "thorn in the flesh" which kept him humble before God. Hazel likewise disciplines his flesh with the metal thorns of three strands of barbed wire wrapped around his chest.[127] These harsh measures do eventually convert him into a beam of redemptive light at the novel's conclusion. In fact, O'Connor has Haze finally recognize the truth behind Jesus' teaching in Matthew 18:9 (a particularly favorite passage of the evangelical white South) that it is better "to enter into life with one eye [or, in Hazel's case, with no eyes] rather than having two eyes to be cast into hell fire." Hazel's self-mutilation allows O'Connor to emphasize two crucial components of the white South's redemption-oriented theology: first, Hazel's blindness eliminates the distractions which have so long kept him from surrendering to Jesus' pursuit; secondly, he gains a more intense spiritual vision allowing him to see what he is now running toward and not from. As Mrs. Flood notices after Hazel rubs quicklime and water into his face, his eyes reveal a "peculiar pushing look, as if [he] were going forward after something [he]

---

126 Ibid, 108.
127 Giannone, *Flannery O'Connor and the Mystery of Love*, 13.

could just distinguish in the distance."[128] While Hazel's means of salvation are extremely Catholic (i.e. through his penitential acts), the evangelical call that leads to his conversion is highly Protestant.

An important distinction should be made between Saul/Paul and Hazel, however. While both men bicker with Christianity, their motives could not be farther apart. Theologian Martin Hengel observes that Saul/Paul persecuted the early Christian community "in the firm conviction that in so doing he was acting according to God's law and will, in zeal for this law."[129] The newly founded cult of Jesus was highly critical of the Mosaic law, leading to the eventual stoning of one of the church's most influential leaders, Stephen (Acts 7:55-60). Saul held the cloaks of the men who stoned Stephen, and seemingly spurred on by this action, he began to persecute the early church in Jerusalem and surrounding areas, imprisoning believers (Acts 8). Haze, on the contrary, denigrates Christianity not because he sees himself as fulfilling God's law but because he wants to deny that there even is a God.

Once Hazel has blinded himself, he begins his journey "backwards to Bethlehem,"[130] drawing toward a spiritual union with Christ as he approaches death. Hazel's journey has truly come full circle now with his end fully recognizable in his beginning. *Wise Blood* opens and closes with the *memento mori* images of death in life that Hazel's surrender to Christ fully embodies within the white South's salvation oriented theology. O'Connor describes the "plain and insistent"[131] outline of a skull under Hazel's skin on the novel's first page, and on its last, the same *memento mori* fuses with the description of Hazel's eyes, his

---

[128] *Wise Blood*, 110-11.
[129] Martin Hengel, *The Pre-Christian Paul*, 65.
[130] *Wise Blood*, 113.
[131] Ibid, 3.

hyper-acute organ of spiritual sight: "The outline of a skull was plain under his skin and the deep burned eye sockets seemed to lead into the dark tunnel where he had disappeared."[132] Hazel's self-blinding, which bestows upon him a theological "tunnel-vision," and his other penitential acts lead to a union with Jesus as he becomes the "pin point of light" that Mrs. Flood had detected in his sightless eyes. It is this dark tunnel that leads him back to Bethlehem and his soul-saving encounter with Christ.

Wise Blood is O'Connor's evangelical project, and Hazel's blindness is her metaphor for the occlusion of humanity's spiritual sight. But the text of *Wise Blood* itself might be said to possess a blind spot; O'Connor is so intent upon demonstrating the machinations of Christian grace that the Southern white church's verticalist tendencies are replicated in *Wise Blood*. The extent of O'Connor's identification with the white Protestant South's hierarchy of heavenly concerns over earthly ones is suggested by her refusal to meet James Baldwin in Georgia in the spring of 1959. To use O'Connor's own words, it "just wouldn't do" for a white woman (regardless of the fact that O'Connor never considered herself a real Southern "lady") to meet with a black writer of the stature and reputation of James Baldwin to discuss art. She explained her reasons for not meeting with Baldwin in a letter to Maryat Lee: "No I can't see James Baldwin in Georgia. It would cause the greatest trouble and disturbance and disunion. In New York it would be nice to meet him; here it would not. I observe the traditions of the society I feed on—it's only fair." O'Connor concluded by saying that one "might as well expect a mule to fly" as for her to see Baldwin within the state borders of Georgia.[133] Even in short stories, such as "The Artificial Nigger" and "Revelation," where her focus seems to be explicitly upon Southern race relations, O'Connor's stories demonstrate an

---

132 Ibid, 120.
133 O'Connor, *The Habit of Being*, 320.

emphasis upon her white main characters' "moments of grace," and Southern blacks are just the impetus of her white characters' "salvation," as in the case of Mrs. Turpin.

In a recent attempt to deal with the question of race in O'Connor's short fiction, one of her most theologically sympathetic critics, Ralph Wood, examines her correspondence with Maryat Lee and concludes that "Flannery O'Connor often sounds like an unabashed racist in her privately expressed opinions."[134] However, he goes on to differentiate between what she wrote in her letters and the purer expressions of her fiction. Wood finds that her fiction offers "the way of the Cross" as the only viable solution to "race hatred."[135] This seems to me to be a strange dichotomy that allows Wood, like O'Connor and much of the rest of her audience, to deflect social concerns with theological ones. As he says, in a statement that sounds as much like O'Connor as anything she wrote herself, "the liberal estimate of human nature is mistaken in the most fundamental way. It ignores the enduring reality of Original Sin, especially in its power to infect the racially righteous no less than the racially sinful."[136] In essence, Wood, in the classic rhetorical gesture of O'Connor's partisan critics, once again replicates the white South's response to racial inequality: why concern ourselves with racial inequality in the here-and-now when everything will be remedied in the hereafter? To paraphrase Paul in the New Testament, O'Connor might have been forced to live *in* the world, but she zealously refuses to be *of* the world, especially the South's racial struggles, which *Wise Blood* (and most of its critics) so studiously avoids.

---

[134] Ralph C. Wood, "Where Is the Voice Coming From?: Flannery O'Connor on Race," 92.

[135] Ibid.

[136] Ibid, 100.

CHAPTER THREE

"OLD DISASTERS AND NEWER HOPES": INTERPRETIVE COMMUNITIES IN WILLIAM FAULKNER'S *LIGHT IN AUGUST*

There is some one myth for every man, which, if we but knew it, would make us understand all that he thought and did.
— William Butler Yeats

If one reads Faulkner without going back to the Bible, to the Old Testament, to the Gospels, to the American society of the period and to his own hallucinatory experience, I believe one cannot reconstitute the complexity of the text itself.
— Julia Kristeva

Contrary to widespread popular belief, ...the persistence of lynching in the region down to the present has not been due simply and wholly to the white-trash classes.... I have myself known university bred men who confessed proudly to having helped roast a Negro.
— W. J. Cash

TO JUSTIFY ITS proclivity toward racial violence, the white South created several myths which took their genesis from the region's iconic book, the Bible. From the parallels between Joe Christmas and Jesus Christ, to the numerous preacher and prophet figures in the novel, to the text's invocation of the white South's racist biblical hermeneutic, William Faulkner's *Light in August* intertextually challenges the white South's dominant religious ideology. *Light in August* intertextually summons elements of the white South's religiosity so that Faulkner might engage in a dialogue (through allusion, parody, silent quotation, and appropriation) with the social context of the white South's gospel, a curious combination of religion and racism.[137] Whereas O'Connor's *Wise Blood* replicates the verticalist theology of many white Southerners, Faulkner examines the white South's intertwining of racism and biblical hermeneutical practice. The dialogue between Faulkner's novel and the Bible (and its attendant white institutions) is a powerful literary and cultural criticism, which forces readers to reexamine the ways the white South appropriated the Bible to justify its racism.[138]

Some readers have puzzled over the differences between Faulkner's characters and the biblical figures they invoke. For example, H. L. Weathersby asks if the divergences between the Yoknapatawpha chronicles and their antecedent biblical stories reveal in Faulkner a combination of "a more than common

---

[137] In her *Faulkner's Un-Christlike Christians: Biblical Allusions in the Novels*, Jessie Coffee identifies thirty-four direct, easily recognizable allusions to the Bible in *Light in August* (129) but does not take into account the numerous other intertexts that indicate the novel's interaction with the South's religiosity nor the implicit critique of such an intertextual practice.

[138] Alan Nadel makes a similar point about the critical nature of literary allusions in "Translating the Past: Literary Allusions as Covert Criticism," but he stops short of considering the larger societal or ideological implications possible within the notion of intertextuality.

knowledge of traditional Christian images...with...a more than common ignorance of Christian doctrine and theology."[139] Weathersby's answer to his own question is that "the theological dimension in the novels is muddled not for any deliberate artistic reason."[140] On the contrary, I assert that Faulkner's biblical allusions do not represent shoddy craftsmanship but are the site of an intertextual confrontation with one of the South's powerful "interpretive communities,"[141] that is, the element within white Southern Protestantism that turned to the Bible to justify its racist practices. In these early twentieth-century white interpretive communities, the Bible was not considered in the historical and cultural contexts which helped generate it, but was naturalized to the interpreters' world and made to render incontrovertible statements on community concerns.[142] These interpretive communities may or may not be drawn along denominational lines, but members of such a community arrive at similar answers to questions asked of the Bible. In the early twentieth-century white South, interpretative communities existed over concerns such as dancing, card playing, drinking, attending movies, and swimming on Sundays.

One of the white South's more influential interpretive communities sought justifications from the Bible for maintaining African-Americans "in their proper place."[143] By putting African-

---

[139] H L. Weathersby, "Supten's Garden," 354.

[140] Ibid, 356.

[141] In *Biblical Interpretation*, Robert Morgan and John Barton apply Stanley Fish's concept of "interpretive communities" to biblical studies, drawing attention to the ways in which various Christian sects are composed of believers who agree to read the Bible according to shared assumptions (257-60).

[142] Edgar V. McKnight, *The Bible and the Reader: An Introduction to Literary Criticism*, xi-xii.

[143] See Cain Hope Felder's "Race, Racism, and the Biblical Narratives" for an investigation of common racially motivated readings of the Bible. Felder comes to the conclusion that "the Bible contains no narratives in

Americans in this segregated and alienated "place," the white South performed a vital act of self-definition. Blacks and "blackness" were defined by one criteria: black was anyone (or anything, such as an act or deed) which was *"not white."*[144] To these racially prejudiced interpretive communities seeking to justify their beliefs and practices, blacks *represent "the other half* of the racially divided world," forming an "antithesis or a counterpoint to the white world."[145] The juxtaposition of the Bible and its promulgating institutions and ministers with Faulkner's fictional world "begets"[146] a third text in the reader's imagination. This new text is then a damning indictment of the interpretive community's attempts to seek a divine sanction for the white South's gospel of racial discrimination. What Weathersby perceives as being muddled actually often emerges in Faulkner's writing as an ironic gap between his reworking of the Christian stories and the actual debased practices for which these same stories are employed in the Southern gospel of racism.

One of the critics who has been most helpful in determining Faulkner's participation within the South's cultural context is Eric J. Sundquist. *In Faulkner: The House Divided*, Sundquist examines race in the Yoknapatawpha novels and advises critics to keep Faulkner's personal comments on race relations and segregation in proper focus when examining his fiction because taking them too lightly "divorce[s] his fiction from the realities it constantly sought to incorporate," and taking them too seriously would easily "convict Faulkner of a lapse in moral vision." Rather, Sundquist maintains that critics should view these statements as

---

which the original intent was to negate the full humanity of black people or view blacks in an unfavorable way. Such negative attitudes about black people are entirely postbiblical" (127).

[144] Thadious Davis, *Faulkner's "Negro": Art and the Southern Context*, 14.
[145] Ibid, 3.
[146] Michel Grisset, "Introduction: Faulkner Between the Texts," 6.

expressing "both a defiance [of] and a tragic sympathy"[147] for the white South's prevailing expressions of racial intolerance. This advice seems sound, for Faulkner made many confusing and contradictory statements regarding the South's racial inequalities, espousing both a "defiance" of the white South's racial practices and a residual "sympathy" for its unwillingness to abandon what he saw as a quickly fading way of life.

These two extremes — defiance and sympathy — mark the emotional poles between which Conservative Southerners often traveled. Historian Joel Williamson describes the Southern white positions of Conservative, Liberal, and Radical in his study or race and race-mixing in America, *A Rage for Order*. While the "Liberals" of Joel Williamson's conception of the Southern "mentalities" on race are characterized by a belief in the unlimited upward potential of African-Americans (a position not found in any of *Light in August*'s characters) and "Radicals" by a belief in a limitless degeneracy outside of the "civilizing" influence of slavery (a position exemplified by the male Burdens, Doc Hines, and Percy Grimm), Conservatives are distinguished by their comparatively moderate position on race. While perhaps acknowledging some of the evils of segregation and discrimination, they realize whites' vested interests in the Jim Crow South and are, at best, grudgingly willing to overturn some of the injustices blacks suffered as second-class citizens.[148] The advantage of the term "Conservative" to describe Faulkner's racial outlook lies not in categorizing him within a large group of Southerners or with justifying his beliefs or actions; rather, such a term provides readers a larger social network within which to place the author and his response to the South's racial intolerance.

In a 1956 interview with Russell Howe, Faulkner displayed a deep ambivalence over the situation of Southern blacks, sounding

---

147 Eric J. Sundquist, *In Faulkner: The House Divided*, 65.
148 Joel Williamson, *Rage for Order*, 70.

many of the keynotes of a Southern racial Conservative. Faulkner did admit that the white South was in the wrong on the civil rights question of the twentieth century as it was in the nineteenth century on the question of slavery. At one point, he stressed his seeming compassion for blacks, emphasizing to Howe, "The Negroes are right—make sure you've got that—they're right.... I've always been on their [the Negroes'] side." He went on to say, "I will go on saying Southerners are wrong and that their position is untenable."[149] However, Faulkner, as revealed in several other comments from this same interview, apparently drew a distinction between "untenable" positions, those of the white South, and indefensible positions, those of the meddlesome federal government and "outside" civil rights agitators. He seemed to possess similar attitudes to many other white Southerners, including Flannery O'Connor: the dangerous result of such agitation would be the eventual alliance of moderate, conservative whites, such as himself, with more extreme, radical, and potentially violent white supremacists. Faulkner succinctly expressed this opinion when he claimed, "As long as there's a middle road, all right. I'll be on it. But if it came to fighting I'd fight for Mississippi against the United States even if it meant going out into the street and shooting Negroes."[150] As a sanction for this claim, Faulkner invoked the South's knight chevalier, Robert E. Lee, equating his choice of Mississippi over the United States to Lee's reluctant choice of Virginia over the Union in 1861.[151] The editors of *Lion in the Garden*, James B. Meriwether and Michael Millgate, maintain that this interview "must be treated with considerable caution because the two published versions differ from one another"[152] and because Faulkner repudiated parts

---

[149] William Faulkner, *Lion in the Garden: Interviews with William Faulkner*, 262.

[150] Ibid, 260-61.

[151] Ibid, 262.

[152] Ibid, 257.

of it, claiming that it contains "statements which no sober man would make, nor, it seems to me, any sane man believe."[153]

In his biography of Faulkner, Blotner addresses the question of Faulkner's sobriety, mentioning that Faulkner had been drinking heavily during this period because of anxiety over the potential violence surrounding the admittance of Autherine Lucy to the University of Alabama. On the other hand, Blotner maintains that Saxe Commins, in whose office the interview took place, does not dispute any of the statements attributed to Faulkner in this interview. Faulkner, in most of his pronouncements on the South's racial problems, characterized his stance as a "go-slow" policy, a key Conservative phrase that allows the potential for movement between the rhetoric of racial harmony and un-Reconstructed Southerner. Faulkner passed away just months before the "Battle of Oxford" over the admission of James Meredith to the University of Mississippi, a battle he probably would have seen as the tragic result of increased meddlesome federal intervention. Changes in the South's racial system might be inevitable, but the harsh example of Reconstruction taught white Southerners that federally imposed change undermined their position of superiority.

Faulkner's comments on the white South's religiosity allow for the same latitude of movement as those he made on Southern race relations. Regardless of his standing in Oxford churches, Faulkner heeded the white South's admonition to study the Bible. The Southern ideology of piety and zeal nearly permeated Oxford as indicated by a 1907 religious census revealing that "there were only 180 unconverted persons in the community, two-thirds of this number being under the age of 12 years."[154] Faulkner assimilated his early religious training from both the Baptist denomination and the Methodist denomination, the church to

---

[153] Ibid, 265.
[154] Joseph Blotner, *Faulkner: A Biography*, 16.

which his family belonged and into which he was baptized. Among the town's most faithful attendants of Methodist Sunday services and annual camp meetings was Faulkner's mother, who took her son with her, while his grandmother would sometimes take him to the Baptist church.[155] As a boy, Faulkner not only attended church but was also expected to follow the Prime Imperative of Protestantism and study the scriptures. One family member holding him to this task was the stern and imposing figure of his great-grandfather, Dr. John Young Murry, who expected everyone who sat down to a meal with him, from children to adults, to recite a Bible verse before eating.[156] Faulkner's church attendance decreased after about the age of twelve as he began to prefer spending time at his father's livery stable and pursuing other Southern masculine pastimes, such as hunting. After his marriage to Estelle Oldham, the Faulkners could best be described as infrequent church attendees, usually only making an appearance at Oxford's St. Peter's Episcopal church on religious holidays.[157] While his adult church attendance record was poor at best, Faulkner never failed to execute the Protestant Prime Imperative, saying that he remained a student and reader of the Bible all his life.[158] He even invested in a fourteen-volume Cambridge edition of the Bible, including the Apocrypha, an edition normally used by biblical scholars.[159]

Despite his early religious training and his continued Bible study, one would be hard-pressed to claim any narrowly conceived Christian orthodoxy for Faulkner, especially an orthodoxy meeting the approval of the dominant Southern

---

[155] Ibid, 21.

[156] Faulkner, *Lion in the Garden*, 250.

[157] Blotner, *Faulkner: A Biography*, 483.

[158] Faulkner, *Lion in the Garden*, 284.

[159] Joseph Blotner, *William Faulkner's Library: A Catalogue*, 87.

Protestant sects.[160] When asked by a University of Virginia student about the proliferation of biblical imagery in his works, Faulkner replied: "Remember, the writer must write out of his background. He must write out of what he knows and *the Christian legend is part of any Christian's background, especially the background of a country boy*, a Southern country boy. My life was passed, my childhood, in a very small Mississippi town, and that was part of my background. I grew up with that. I assimilated that, took that in without even knowing it"[161] (emphasis added). What Faulkner utilized to create his mythical county was not so much doctrine as narrative, using what he called the "Christian legend" as an intertextual well-spring for his fiction. The fundamental value of the Christian stories for Faulkner was their ability to teach humanity its potential. He once said that the Bible "shows [mankind] how to discover himself, evolve for himself a moral code and standard within his capacities and aspirations by giving him a matchless example of suffering and sacrifice and the promise of hope."[162] Perhaps the clearest formulation of Faulkner's religious sensibility can be found in John W. Hunt's *William Faulkner: Art in Theological Tension*. Hunt concludes that Faulkner accepted the Christian view of the universe as a place where evil has very real effects and that man is in some sense fallen; however, Faulkner does not display a belief in the Christian tenet of redemption through supernatural agency.[163] While this "promise of hope" is obvious throughout Faulkner's fiction, *Light in August* also shows its author borrowing from the Bible to

---

[160] Evans Harrington, in "Religion and Faulkner's Art," comes to a similar conclusion regarding Faulkner's relationship with Protestant Christianity (161-62).

[161] Frederick Gwynn and Joseph Blotner, eds, *Faulkner in the University: Class Conferences at the University of Virginia, 1957-1958*, 87.

[162] Faulkner, *Lion in the Garden*, 247.

[163] John W. Hunt, *William Faulkner: Art in Theological Tension*, 22.

demonstrate the white South's failure to live up to its self-proclaimed "moral code."

Despite Faulkner's own revealing statements, several critics have attempted to claim orthodox doctrinal beliefs for Faulkner, with Cleanth Brooks being perhaps the most influential. Brooks concludes "Faulkner's Ultimate Values" by claiming that "Faulkner's conception of the human being is thus right in the mainstream of the great classical-Judaic-Christian tradition."[164] As John N. Duvall has observed, such pronouncements have long dominated the majority of Faulkner criticism.[165] Views such as Brooks's, which so completely identify Faulkner with the Christian norms of his community, pose the potential danger of deflecting the critical thrust of a text like *Light in August*. Faulkner's work could easily be seen as simply replicating the white South's web of religion and racism. On the contrary, Joe Christmas, or more specifically, the community's discursive response to Joe Christmas, is fundamental to *Light in August's* critique of the Southern synthesis of racism and religion. Christmas comes to occupy a somewhat analogous position with Christ[166] because both become living embodiments of language's generative, creative power. Christ was the incarnate Word or Logos made flesh who dwelt among humanity, and Joe Christmas

---

[164] Cleanth Brooks, "Faulkner's Ultimate Values," 28.

[165] John N. Duvall, "Murder and the Communities: Ideology In and Around *Light in August*," 101.

[166] C. Hugh Holman, in his outstanding examination of the parallels between Christmas's life and Christ's, "The Unity of *Light in August*," argues that Faulkner patterned Christmas after what might be called the "Suffering Servant" interpretive community (158). Not only does Holman's argument account for why some events from the life of Christ are re-enacted in that of Christmas (i.e. those which reinforce the view of Christ as Suffering Servant), but it also raises the question of what is emphasized in biblical hermeneutics. The South's interpretive communities must emphasize certain portions of the biblical text over others.

embodies the racist interpretive community's discourse. Christ is the Word of God, His "only begotten Son"[167] and yet a man who walked among men and women; whereas Joe becomes the word "nigger," the construct of the community's racist language. In the Gospel of John's invocation of the Genesis story of creation, the Word is the means by which everything is created: "In the beginning was the Word, and the Word was with God, and the Word was God. The same was in the beginning with God. All things were made by Him; and without Him was not anything made that was made."[168] The opening phrase, "In the beginning," and the Greek term "Logos" hearken back to God's construction of the universe. God created the cosmos by speaking the phrase, "Let there be...." God pronounces all of His creation to be "good," particularly His Son whom he blesses through the symbolic descent of a dove. However, Christmas's rhetorical construction by the racist interpretive community is to make him the villain, the embodiment of evil which must be exorcised.

Language is used to determine Joe, to create his identity within the community, only now the all-defining Word becomes the racial slur, "nigger." When he arrives in Jefferson, Christmas appears to be a white man, and, though he performs "nigger-work" at the mill, no one attaches such a label to him personally. As one would expect in a community concerned with policing racial purity and exposing hidden violations of communal strictures, Joe's initial appearance, however, does raise doubts regarding his racial identity. As one man at the mill asks, "Did you ever hear of a white man named Christmas?"[169] However, these misgivings are easily overcome by assigning Joe the status of "foreigner," and Christmas is not yet stigmatized as the town's

---

[167] John 3:16.
[168] John 1:1-3.
[169] *Light in August*, 20.

ultimate Other, the most fearsome thing Jefferson, and the South, could imagine.

When this labeling does occur, when Jefferson eventually defines Joe as black and loathsome, the community also defines itself. As long as there is a Joe Christmas to embody everything the community finds reprehensible, then the townspeople can clearly proclaim themselves acceptable, harmonious elements of their society. This violent process of establishing social definitions is foreshadowed earlier in the novel. Joe proclaims himself as not "womanly" and weak like his adoptive mother when he participates in the sexual initiation with the black woman in the shed, and then rejects others' designations of himself as "black" by violently attacking the woman who offers herself to the five boys. In much the same way, the white citizens of Jefferson declare their communal identity through their discursive practices and eventual violence. "To merge white and black would have been the ultimate holocaust, the ultimate damnation of Southern civilization. And yet that was precisely what the mulatto, by his very being, represented."[170]

Faulkner carefully revised the text of *Light in August* to remove all definite clues pertaining to Christmas' racial identity.[171] Joe carries within himself the secret of his indeterminate heritage and tells only two people in Jefferson of his belief that he may be of mixed racial ancestry: Joanna Burden and Lucas Burch, both of whom play key roles in the community's discursive definition of Joe. While Burden believes Joe to be black, she tells no one her lover's secret. Instead, Brown first affixes this label to Christmas; "Accuse the white and let the nigger run," he proclaims during the sheriff's interrogation. The sheriff, skeptical at first of Brown's

---

[170] Joel Williamson, *New People: Miscegenation and Mulattoes in the United States*, 95.

[171] Regina K. Fadiman, *Faulkner's Light in August: A Description and Interpretation of the Revisions*, 125.

revelation, warns him to be careful of his accusation, saying, "You better be careful what you are saying, if it is a white man you are talking about.... I dont care if he is a murderer or not,"[172] but then concludes that his prisoner is "telling the truth at last."[173] Killing can be honorable in Jefferson, as when Colonel Sartoris kills two Burdens to prevent African-American voting, or when Doc Hines murders his granddaughter's lover because of his supposed black blood. These killings are justifiable—to the white community—because they preserve dominant communal racial values.

To white Jefferson, only one thing is worse than being a "nigger" and that is being a "nigger" who murders one of the emblems of Southern ideology, a white woman. Though Jefferson ostracized Joanna during her lifetime because of the abolitionist sins of her fathers, once she is murdered "she becomes as white and respectable and Southern as the communal hysteria requires."[174] As Philip Weinstein has noticed, a typical transformation occurs after the sheriff believes Brown and the "knowledge" of Christmas's black ancestry is leaked to the community: "Pronounce the word nigger and Joanna Burden's murder becomes a rape...." In the South, "racism proceeds... through discursive insistence."[175]

---

172 *Light in August*, 91.
173 Ibid, 92.
174 Sundquist, *In Faulkner: The House Divided*, 84.
175 Philip Weinstein, *Faulkner's Subject: A Cosmos No One Owns*, 51. A similar type of communal insistence is depicted in "Dry September," the story of another lynching in Jefferson triggered by a supposed sexual attack upon a white woman. In the story, the town is easily swept into a vigilante frenzy because of a spinster's claims who has a history of fabricating stories about attacks upon her sexual virtue. Like *Light in August*, the townspeople of Jefferson, with the notable exception of Hawkshaw, are quick to read the situation in terms of Will Mayes's black skin. Regardless of either his past humility or service to the white townspeople, his societal position as "nigger" guarantees his guilt. "Dry September" was published in 1931, a year before *Light in August*.

Several characters in *Light in August* serve as self-ordained mouthpieces for the Southern interpretative community's gospel of prejudice. First is Calvin Burden, Sr., who, like Simon McEachern, attempts to inculcate his religious values into his family through domestic violence, promising that he would "beat the loving God into" them as long as he was strong enough to raise his arm.[176] Though not born in the South, Burden and his son, Nathaniel, appropriate one of the region's most commonly held biblical sanctions for racial hatred: the myth of Ham's curse. If this twisted hermeneutical strategy did not originate in the South, it certainly received a hearty endorsement there. Nathaniel Burden's advocacy of this justification is revealed when, speaking to his daughter Joanna, he characterizes blacks as living under a "curse which God put on [the] whole race before your grandfather or your brother or me or you were even thought of."[177]

Burden pronounces all African-Americans to be "lowbuilt black folks: lowbuilt because of the weight of the wrath of God, black because of the sin of human bondage staining their blood and flesh."[178] He is alluding to the story of Ham, his brothers, Shem and Japheth, and their father, Noah, as recounted in Genesis 9:20-26.

> And Noah began to be an husbandman, and he planted a vineyard: And he drank of the wine, and was drunken; and he was uncovered within his tent. And Ham, the father of Canaan, saw the nakedness of his father, and told his two brethren without. And Shem and Japheth took a garment, and laid it upon both their shoulders, and went backward, and covered the nakedness of their father; and their faces were backward, and they saw not their father's nakedness. And Noah awoke from his wine, and knew what his younger son had done unto him. And

---

[176] *Light in August*, 230.
[177] Ibid, 239.
[178] Ibid, 234.

he said, *Cursed be Canaan, a servant of servants shall he be unto his brethren.*[179]

The myth of Ham as a justification for slavery and, later, for institutional and personal racism enjoyed great popularity throughout the entire region.[180] As Thomas Virgil Peterson argues in *Ham and Japheth: The Mythic World of Whites in the Antebellum South*, the myth of Ham was so powerful because it seemed to come directly from the Bible, the South's secure anchor for its intertwining web of racism and religion. Out of this Genesis story, the South extrapolated an elaborate mythical justification for enslaving and segregating blacks. While Shem and Japheth cover their father's nakedness, the white South believed that Ham commits some ambiguous sin while viewing the naked patriarch. For his transgression, Ham and his offspring on into perpetuity are sentenced to be "servant[s] of servants" to his brothers. Perhaps the most important result of Ham's transgression is that he is excluded from his tribal nation's patriarchal power structure. In much the same way, because they were viewed as the children of Ham, African-Americans' biblical interpretive communities were either excluded from or denigrated by the interpretive practices of the white South.[181]

Based upon its appeals to these few biblical verses, the South embellished this myth until it explained the most widely perceived differences and inferiorities of blacks. For example, blacks had darker skin because God placed His mark upon Ham

---

[179] See Forrest G. Wood's *The Arrogance of Faith: Christianity and Race in America from the Colonial Era to the Twentieth Century* for another discussion of the myth of Ham. Wood traces the history and development of this biblical justification.

[180] See Winthrop D. Jordan's *White Over Black* for a detailed examination of the proliferation of race prejudice in the white American mind in the years before the Civil War.

[181] Virgil Peterson, *Ham and Japheth: The Mythic World of Whites in the Antebellum South*, 78.

and his family to distinguish them as the race of servants. The white Southern racist interpretive community strongly believed in an omniscient and infallible God; therefore, this wise God must have provided a designation, a mark, to indicate exactly who belonged to this group of social and moral inferiors—despite the fact that the mark is not mentioned in the actual Bible verses.

Many commentators on this myth highlighted the sexual nature of Ham's sin. Though Nathan Lord and John Fletcher, leading proponents of the myth, could not specify what exactly Ham's sin was, they and many of their followers agreed that it involved some violation of God's laws of sexual purity.[182] Members of the white interpretive community—like Burden, Sr., who thinks blacks descended from Ham—believed that African-Americans proved they came from their allegedly licentious forefather by virtue of their continued insatiable sexual appetites and sexual aggression. Zora Neale Hurston lampooned this white interpretation of Ham's curse in her one-act play, "The First One"; the "first one" of her title referring to Ham as the first black person. While Hurston revels in dismantling one of the myths that helped prop up the white South's stereotypes of African-Americans, *Light in August* reveals the deadly earnestness with which racist interpretive communities adopted this myth. It is, after all, the perception of Joe as black, and therefore as one of Ham's descendants, that allows Jefferson to quickly equate Joanna's murder with sexual violation. Once Christmas is convicted of the killing *and* of being a cursed descendant of Ham, he is then incapable of resisting the temptation to soil the most highly regarded emblem of the South's ideology of racial purity, a white woman.

For the Burden men who take upon themselves the task of interpreting God's Word, the Bible is a poorly understood document whose only seemingly transparent passages attest to

---

[182] Ibid.

God's eternal vindictiveness toward blacks (after all, the semi-literate Calvin Burden, Sr. reads from the Bible in a language, Spanish, which none of his children comprehends). For Doc Hines, the last, and most malignant, of *Light in August's* "preachers" of racist dogma, the Bible as a physical object is only of peripheral importance. Instead of quoting the Bible or common interpretations of its stories, Doc Hines presumes to speak for God, assuming for himself the power of an Old Testament prophet emerging from the wilderness, filled with the righteous indignation of a Jeremiah. In this respect, he represents the logical extension of the South's racially dogmatic biblical interpretive community. While the Burden men insidiously interpret key Bible passages, especially the myth of Ham, Doc's single concern with the Bible is with the message it delivers to him on black inferiority; he reads the Bible *only* through the lens of his own racism. He uses this hermeneutical tactic as an authorization to deliver his racist message straight into the heart of Southern African-American society, its churches, entering "the pulpit and in his harsh, dead voice and at times with violent obscenity, preach[ing] to them humility before all skins lighter than theirs, preaching the superiority of the white race, himself his own exhibit A."[183] He is the literal personification of the white South's racist biblical hermeneutic against whom Hurston and Wright's characters will pit their voices.

Doc Hines assumes this role of God's spokesman, or "His chosen instrument"[184] as he prefers to call himself, when dealing with both blacks and whites. While questioning the orphanage dietitian, Doc pours out what he feels to be God's hatred against "bitchery and abomination,"[185] sounding much like the "Thus Saith The LORD" of the Old Testament prophets railing against

---

183 *Light in August*, 325.
184 Ibid, 365.
185 Ibid, 341.

Israel's wickedness. And like a true prophet, he not only communicates God's message to the people, but Doc also spurs the masses into taking action. As Gavin Stevens reports, it is Doc Hines who stands on the street corners of Jefferson "preaching lynching"[186] and exhorting the community to take their final retribution upon Joe Christmas. The raw hatred Doc Hines displays toward Christmas, his own grandson, is different only in degree, not in kind, from what the rest of the community feels toward Joe. Doc Hines has fully absorbed the white South's racial gospel, particularly its Old Testament-like predilection for pronouncing curses.

The curse of Ham was hereditary because the white racist interpretive community maintained that it was passed from generation to generation through blood.[187] The South's dogmatic, insistent endorsement of the blood myth is reflected as Doc seeks out Milly's lover and murders him because the old man believes God has revealed to him "that the fellow had nigger blood."[188] Again, Doc's faith in the white South's gospel of racism is different in degree, not in kind, from the white community's whole-hearted belief that Christmas has "nigger blood" in him after Burch makes his confession. John Mencke, in *Mulattoes and Race Mixture*, asserts that the foundation of the "one-drop rule" was laid in the early 1800s. The one-drop rule clearly stated that one drop of black blood in a person's veins made him or her black. Of course "blackness" in individuals was inextricably connected to sexual

---

[186] Ibid, 423.

[187] At the Nagano Conference, Faulkner referred to the white South's belief that race characteristics were transmitted through the blood as a "delusion" On this occasion, Faulkner went on to make the argument that the basis of racial conflict in the South was economic and that many moral smoke screens (such as the concept of blood differences) were offered to deflect attention away from these economic considerations (Faulkner, *Lion in the Garden*, 183).

[188] *Light in August*, 354.

taboos, and the one-drop rule was enforced to protect the virtue of Southern white womanhood as emblem of Southern purity and as property of the white Southern male. As Charles Staples Mangum, Jr. declared, "If it is known that an individual has the least modicum of Negro blood, then he or she is considered a suitable mate of colored persons only."[189] The one-drop rule became "fact" when pseudo-scientists began to theorize not only that blood was the transmission agent for individual characteristics but that entire races demonstrated identifiable properties which were carried in their blood.[190] By the early twentieth century, faith in blood as a transmitter of racial characteristics was unshakable. For the white South, race as ideological construct determines behavior.

Black blood represented a stain (with all of that word's connotations about physical and moral contamination) as evidenced by one South Carolina woman who received a court affidavit in the mid-1800s to pronounce her blood pure and free of any color taint.[191] Josiah Priest, writing as early as 1843, neatly summed up the notions of black, corrupted blood which would have currency well into the twentieth century South when he stated, "The baleful fire of unchaste amour rages through the negro's blood, more fiercely than in the blood of any other people."[192] As one historian has put it, by the end of the nineteenth and the beginning of the twentieth centuries, the concept of blood "attained the proportions of an article of faith"[193] in the South. The phrase "article of faith" is significant because it suggests the religious zeal with which the South stood by this abstraction.[194]

---

[189] Quoted in Williamson, *New People*, 98.

[190] John G. Mencke, *Mulattoes and Race Mixture*, 37-87.

[191] Jordan, *White Over Black*, 166.

[192] George M. Fredrickson, *The Black Image in the White Mind*, 276.

[193] Jordan, *White Over Black*, 167.

[194] See René Girard's *Violence and the Sacred* (36-38) for a discussion of the dual functions of blood as both purifier and stain in religious discourse.

While the male Burdens and Doc Hines represent the most vitriolic members of the white South's racist interpretative community, Simon McEachern represents another common response to the region's intertwining tendrils of race and religion. McEachern, and those like him, remains silent when facing the dilemma of reconciling Christian faith and unjust social practices. Whereas some white Southerners "naturalized" Jim Crow practices with the aid of the region's greatest moral authority, McEachern does not consult the Bible on matters of racial justice, not even negatively, like the Burdens and Doc Hines. McEachern symbolizes the response of many white Southern Protestants — his energy and attention are focused on the other-worldly concerns of personal redemption; therefore, he has little concern for improving material concerns on this earth, particularly those of a race widely considered to be inferior by most white Southern Protestants.[195] In this respect, McEachern reveals himself to be the spiritual kinsman of Hazel Motes of Flannery O'Connor's *Wise Blood*; both pursue their salvation to the exclusion of societal considerations. All he has taught his foster-son is a long list of "Shalt Not['s]"[196] from which Joe escapes only when he brings the chair down on McEachern's head. McEachern's religious vision is so fully implicated in perpetuating the status-quo on an individual or personal basis that he could never answer Joe's question of when "will men with different blood stop hating one another?"[197]; in fact, he could never even formulate the question.

Reverend Gail Hightower stands in stark contrast to these lay ministers who either proclaim the twisted gospel of racial hatred or who are unwilling to recognize the white South's racist religious practices. Hightower realizes the full murderous implications of the community's insistence that Christmas has

---

[195] Samuel S. Hill, "Survey of Southern Religious History," 409.
[196] *Light in August*, 194.
[197] Ibid, 236.

black blood in his veins. Sitting in his home, Hightower hears the town's church-bells and, in a moment of prescience, understands that Jefferson will soon lynch Christmas, thinking that "in [this] crucifixion they too will raise a cross."[198] René Girard's thesis from *Violence and the Sacred* reverberates through Hightower's insight. Girard asserts that sacrifices are performed upon "sacrificeable" victims to deflect violence away from a community and knit it even closer together.[199] This connection between Christmas' impending death and Christ's crucifixion is more than a casual reference to the Bible. This intertext reveals the community's consciousness, what Faulkner calls its "collective memory," exposing the town's need to exorcise its greatest communal fears and doubts. As Hightower foretells, Jefferson will lynch Christmas "gladly,...since to pity him would be to admit self-doubt and to hope for and need pity themselves."[200] To respond in any other way would indicate a less than whole-hearted faith in the Southern gospel and reveal misgivings about the self-identity they have created for themselves as members of the white community and the identity they have created for the African-American community. In Thadious Davis's words, Christmas is lynched "to preserve Jefferson as it is,"[201] that is, racially pure and confident that the white community's opposite and corresponding other half poses no threat to their sanctity.

This obsession with racial purity often made the white South fear men of mixed ancestry the most because there was no black skin to correspond with the perceived "black" heart. Despite some notions of mulatto impotency,[202] the sexuality of men of mixed

---

[198] Ibid, 348.

[199] Girard, *Violence and the Sacred*, 4, 1-35.

[200] *Light in August*, 348.

[201] Davis, *Faulkner's "Negro": Art and the Southern Context*, 173.

[202] A few Southerners believed in the so-called notion of the "mule-atto" According to this theory, a mulatto was equated with a mule, both being the offspring of what the South would view as cross-breeding. Just

ancestry was very distressing to the white South because some mulattoes could "pass" as whites. This power to escape detection made the paranoid white South fear that mulattoes were the most frequent violators of the region's primary taboo. In the words of Senator Benjamin Ryan Tillman of South Carolina, Southern white women were virtually besieged by sex-crazed men of tainted blood, their "breast[s] pulsating with the desire to sate their passions upon white maidens and wives.... Forty to one hundred maidens are sacrificed annually to the Minotaur, and there is no Theseus in sight."[203] These alleged mulatto rapists were driven to act as they did because of their blood inheritance from the "wild, naked, man-eating savages of equatorial Africa"[204] whose sexual degeneracy was now a widely held belief. Their potential danger was cloaked because of the difficulty in determining who these "white niggers" were, these men "with black hearts under white skins who might marry [the white South's] daughters, who might by that fact quietly, insidiously rape them."[205] The very existence of mulattoes threatened the South's discursive practices on race because the entire system could break down if whites were no longer able to identify the community's signifier of evil and otherness.

Southern negrophobia and fear of black blood during the late nineteenth and early twentieth centuries caused a new, metaphorical definition of "blackness" and the creation of a new category—the "white nigger." The supposed curse upon Ham's

---

as no mule could reproduce, so it was assumed no mulatto could either. Faulkner was aware of this theory, once saying to Sherwood Anderson, "the cross between the jack and the mare that produced the mule" and its sterility "was just the same" as the cross between "the white man and the Negro woman" (Blotner, *Faulkner: A Biography*, 180). Blotner feels that Faulkner was pulling Anderson's leg, simply telling him some of the quainter and more eccentric Southern notions.

[203] Quoted in Williamson, *Rage for Order*, 84.
[204] Mencke, *Mulattoes and Race Mixture*, 117.
[205] Williamson, *Rage for Order*, 239.

offspring persisted until the early twentieth century, but physiognomy was no longer an accurate test to determine who were members of this cursed race because the offending black blood could have traveled through several white generations. No perceptible trace of African ancestry was necessary to define a person as black. The label "white nigger" was a definition after the fact; some sin or moral failing (often some sexual transgression) proved a person's blackness because no virtuous member of the white community could betray his or her race in such a heinous manner.[206] After a member of the Mottstown crowd brands him with this title, shouting, "Christmas! That white nigger that did that killing,"[207] the community's suspicions are confirmed, and Joe's lynching becomes inevitable. And, as if to add insult to the white community's injury, Joe flouts these beliefs right up until he is captured, going "into a white barbershop like a white man, and because he looked like a white man they never suspected him."[208] Such insolence could not be tolerated. After having this walking violation of their beliefs in their midst for so long, undetected, the townspeople must have vengeance. Jefferson, swayed by all these discursive practices, makes Christmas its most radical expression of its fear of "blackness" because Joe's blackness is internal, detectable only after the fact by his alleged crimes. The community, therefore, responds with the time-honored Southern practice of lynching.[209]

After establishing a link between Joe and the myth of Ham, the town believes Joe's blood to be tainted, a foregone conclusion which receives expression when Grimm castrates Christmas,

---

[206] Ibid.

[207] *Light in August*, 326.

[208] Ibid, 331.

[209] Between the years 1882 and 1927, an era which greatly overlaps with Faulkner's life, 4,951 men, women, and children were lynched, and 3,513 of these victims were African-American (Trudier Harris, *Exorcising Blackness: Historical and Literary Lynching and Burning Rituals*, 7).

declaring, "Now you'll let white women alone, even in hell."[210] The community displays a deadly logic concerning Joe's alleged crime. Joe raped Joanna before murdering her, and maybe even again after murdering her,[211] because he has black blood and that accounts for and explains this heinous crime. Faulkner depicts the ultimate result of this "reasoning" as a violently ironic commentary on Christ's injunction from Matthew 18:7-9 to avoid sin.

> Woe unto the world because of offenses! for it must needs be that offenses come; but woe to that man by whom the offence cometh! Wherefore if thy hand or thy foot offend thee, cut them off, and cast them from thee: it is better for thee to enter into life halt or maimed, rather than having two hands or two feet to be cast into everlasting fire. And if thy eye offend thee, pluck it out, and cast it from thee: it is better for thee to enter into life with one eye, rather than having two eyes to be cast into hell fire.

This biblical passage serves as Hazel Moses's justification for his very individual, self-mutilating quest for salvation in *Wise Blood*, but these same verses have grave consequences for the white community's health in *Light in August*. Joe's mutilation is a symbolic exorcism of the community's evil. As Thadious Davis maintains, "Because Joe is accused of the rape-murder of Joanna Burden and because he is labeled 'nigger' by [Lucas Burch] and consequently hunted as a 'nigger,' Joe dies a nigger's death."[212] As Davis's nearly liturgical repetition of this slur-term indicates, "nigger" is almost religious in its ability to designate Jefferson's most reprehensible element, the hidden evil lurking behind a white facade.

At the close of chapter 19, the reader confronts *Light in August*'s ambiguous comment upon Joe's execution in Hightower's kitchen. Faulkner uses the analogy of a rocket to describe the release of

---

[210] *Light in August*, 439.

[211] Ibid, 272.

[212] Davis, *Faulkner's "Negro": Art and the Southern Context*, 167.

Christmas's blood which has been of such central importance to Jefferson's citizens.

> It seemed to rush out of his pale body like the rush of sparks from a rising rocket; upon that black blast the man seemed to rise soaring into their memories forever and ever. They are not to lose it, in whatever peaceful valleys, beside whatever placid and reassuring streams of old age, in the mirroring faces of whatever children they will contemplate old disasters and newer hopes. It will be there musing, quiet, steadfast, not fading,...of itself alone serene, of itself alone triumphant.[213]

Although Joe's life parallels Christ's, the intertextual intersection of these two stories provides no neat solution to the society's race problem that has been graphically played out in Christmas's life. And yet that is precisely the point. Joe's death reinforces the community's religious belief in black blood; furthermore, the community will pass Joe's story—quiet, steadfast, never fading—down to its children as a communally reinforcing story. The key biblical story that illuminates Jefferson's citizens' reading of Joe's life is the myth of Ham, not the story of Christ's passion, "the crucified shape of pity and love"[214] which Hightower regrets not offering to his congregation.

The ironic distance between Christmas's death as a Christ-like figure and its function as a prop for the community's racist discourse emerges after considering the case of Gavin Stevens. Stevens appears as perhaps the most sensitive, intelligent, and eloquent individual in Faulkner's "postage stamp" of Yoknapatawpha County. He depicts Joe as a victim of a struggle with his racial ancestry, a conflict he describes in the community's racist dogma of feuding black and white blood.

> It was the black blood which swept him by his own desire beyond the aid of any man, swept him up into that ecstasy out of

---

[213] *Light in August*, 440.
[214] Ibid, 462.

a black jungle where life has already ceased before the heart
stops and death is desire and fulfillment. And then the black
blood failed him again, as it must have in crises all his life.... He
merely...ran on and crouched behind that table and defied the
black blood for the last time, as he had been defying it for thirty
years.[215]

Moreover, Stevens' recounting of Christmas's life in many of
the key terms of the racist interpretive community, particularly
the "doctrine of blood," links him with such characters as Percy
Grimm, Doc Hines, and the Burdens through his perpetuation of
the South's racist discursive practices. As Judith Bryant
Wittenberg observes, all of these characters demonstrate "the
text's predominant concern with race as a linguistic and social
construct rather than a biological given, its focus more on the
concept of race that on actual race relations"[216] (emphasis added).

Light in August concludes, however, on a note of guarded
optimism. The story of Lena Grove and Byron Bunch closes the
novel, the comic ending emphasizing the "newer hopes" of
creating a community not implicated in Christmas's death, as the
one they are leaving. Their relationship provides an alternative to
Jefferson's conventional morality that is complicitous in
Christmas's death through its mindless adherence to the notion of
chaste Southern white womanhood. However, readers of *Light in
August* can not escape the fact that Joe and Lena's lives are only
tangentially connected, neither having much of an immediate
impact on the other because of Joe's expulsion from the
community. As Sundquist argues, "the refusal of the novel fully to
integrate Christmas's story into those that surround him is a
function of the fact that his life and his story are identified with

---

[215] Ibid, 425.
[216] Judith Bryant Wittenberg, "Race in Light in August: Wordsymbols
and Obverse Reflections," 146.

mechanisms of segregation and exclusion, with violent expulsion...from...the larger community of human compassion."[217]

So why does Lena receive at least a modicum of pity and
charity from community members such as Byron's landlady (who
feeds Lena and suggests that she stay in the cabin at the Burden
place) and Martha Armstid (who gives her hard-earned egg-
money to Lena for her trip into Jefferson)? Perhaps Lena becomes
an object of (grudging) charity and pity because even though she
violated communal laws on white female chastity, the community
does not believe her guilty of violating its strictest taboo—racial
mixture. Lena is therefore never associated with the white South's
biblical justifications for violence and social exclusion. Instead, the
white community can invoke precedents from the Gospels where
Christ displayed mercy and kindness toward those accused of
sexual transgressions. On the contrary, Joe is so hated and hunted
because he threatens the sanctity of white Southern society and its
common biblical myths. While his "rape" of Joanna Burden and
his incredible surrender in Mottstown verify these myths, his
"parchment" colored skin belies them. Maybe the "tragic, central
idea" of *Light in August* is not, as Faulkner himself once claimed,
that Joe does not "know what he [is]"[218]; maybe the novel's central
tragedy is how the community projects all of its doubts about its
own "blackness" on to Joe because if he is morally tainted then
perhaps they are too.

Jefferson's white community is willing to go to very violent
lengths to guard against what it felt to be an encroaching
"blackness." For instance, Doc Hines kills his granddaughter's
lover because he thinks the young man might possess some moral
taint in his blood. The community sanctions this violence, and Doc
faces no penalty for murder. Surpassing even this communal

---

[217] Eric J. Sundquist, "Faulkner, Race, and the Forms of American
Fiction," 13.

[218] Gwynn and Blotner, eds, *Faulkner in the University*, 72.

sanction is Doc's belief that God endorsed his actions, going so far as to claim that God held the pistol steady while he pulled the trigger.[219] The Ku Klux Klan, self-appointed guardians against "blackness," nearly beat Hightower to death when he appeared to deviate too drastically from the society's norms. Joe's questions regarding his racial ancestry ensure that white Southern society will reject him because he is a threat. However, white racism has so strongly affected him[220] that his brief experiment living with a black woman in the North must be unsuccessful. Joe is nearly destined to never find the kind of strength and affirmation that Hurston finds so prevalent in African-American culture.

The depictions of violence in *Light in August* mark key points of Faulkner's divergence from Hurston, Wright, and especially O'Connor's contributions to the cultural dialogue on the South's intertwining of race and religion. *Wise Blood's* violence is adamantly personal, a metaphor for O'Connor's insistence upon her characters' need for Christian conversion and, by extension, her readers' conversion. In *Uncle Tom's Children*, Richard Wright asserts that white societal violence must be countered with a violence that liberates blacks from Jim Crow lives. Hurston's *Moses, Man of the Mountain* replies to pervasive white violence by imagining an African-American community that, after winning its freedom, might exist outside of violence. The violence of *Light in August*, especially Christmas's death, however, seems unavoidable. Percy Grimm is like the white community's avenging angel and pursues Christmas with help of a supernatural agency, "The Player" who moves him like a figure on a chess-board.

The optimistic reader of *Light in August* is offered little hope that Yoknapatawpha County's citizens will overcome the South's

---

[219] *Light in August*, 356.

[220] See Andre Bleikasten's *The Ink of Melancholy*, particularly 317, for a discussion of white racism's impact upon Joe and how he reproduces that racism.

gospel of racism. The prejudicial interpretive communities use Joe's life, and more importantly, his death, as a continuing rationale for their actions by the novel's conclusion. As M. Nell Sullivan asserts, most citizens of Jefferson participate in this racist interpretive community: "From the most ignorant—Doc Hines and Percy Grimm—to the most educated—Gavin Stevens—all the white citizens believe that black "blood" contaminates its bearer with moral depravity or evil, and that belief in turn stabilizes their own identities in the Yoknapatawpha play of signifiers."[221] Yet, rather than merely replicating the South's biblically "sanctioned" racist discursive practices, Faulkner challenges them by demonstrating how the region's Old Testament zealousness and scapegoating is not tempered by a New Testament grace. His use of biblical intertextuality in *Light in August* demonstrates how the white South used the Bible to debased ends. Instead of functioning as a "moral code and standard" of "suffering and sacrifice and the promise of hope,"[222] the South's iconic book rendered judgements and inescapable curses upon African-Americans. If *Light in August* is to participate to its greatest potential in the ongoing dialogue on Southern race and religion, it is into our memories as readers that Joe must ascend, affecting us so deeply through the tragic example of his death, brought about by the white South's racist interpretive community's rhetorical practices, that we begin with "newer hopes" (440) to envision a time when men with different blood in them will stop hating each other.

In "Faulkner, Race, and Forms of American Fiction," Eric J. Sundquist states that "[a]lthough Faulkner's novels bring to a pitch the literary confrontation with race hatred in the early twentieth century, there are, by the same token, limitations to his vision. The fictional forms achieved by other authors, both black

---

[221] M. Nell Sullivan, "Persons in Pieces: Race and Aphanisis in *Light in August*," 506.

[222] Faulkner, *Lion in the Garden*, 247.

and white, in the way engage and complete those of Faulkner, reaching beyond the world of Yoknapatawpha and giving clearer voice to black lives..."[223] Zora Neale Hurston is one such voice who helps to complete Faulkner's. *Moses, Man of the Mountain* responds to the white South's hatred and violence by offering an alternate vision, looking forward to creating a loving environment distinct from the pervasive religiously sanctioned racial hatred which is critiqued in *Light in August.*

---

[223] Sundquist, "Faulkner, Race, and the Forms of American Fiction," 3.

CHAPTER FOUR:

"TELL OLE PHARAOH TO LET MY PEOPLE GO": COMMUNAL DELIVERANCE IN ZORA NEALE HURSTON'S *MOSES, MAN OF THE MOUNTAIN*

> *In the main, the message the American Christians communicated to the African diaspora was a gospel distorted by an insidious racism and compromised by self-conceit and economic self-interest. It made God a partner to the white man's cupidity and laid on Him a false ordination of human separation and a spurious consignment of a whole people to perpetual indignity rather than lifting His common fatherhood and publishing His commandment to love.*
> — C. Eric Lincoln

> *How might it be possible to make visible those who have been rendered invisible religiously and historically?*
> — Charles Long

ALICE WALKER CONCLUDES her foreword to Robert Hemenway's *Zora Neale Hurston: A Literary Biography* by asserting that African-

Americans constitute a "people," and "a people do not throw their geniuses away. If they do, it is our duty as witnesses for the future to collect them again for the sake of our children. If necessary, bone by bone."[224] Walker is, of course, speaking not only of her own well-documented attempts to mark the grave of her spiritual and artistic predecessor but also of the necessity of Zora Neale Hurston and her work to complete the mosaic of American literatures. Hemenway and Walker speak eloquently of this need to excavate Hurston's writings, and yet the project of excavation is central to nearly all of Hurston's work. Zora Neale Hurston mined the black folk imagination, revealing a distinctly African-American creativity. In *Moses, Man of the Mountain*, Hurston digs deep into the black folk consciousness to exhume one of its central, cultural figures, Moses. She reconfigures "bone by bone" this black folk hero so that her Moses is transmuted from a figure out of a long ago past into a great cultural hero who delivers Southern blacks to a "land flowing with milk and honey." *Moses* is an empowering revoicing of the Exodus story that responds to the white South's racist biblical interpretive communities by appropriating a key figure from the Bible, by intertextually recasting Moses as an African-American liberator. *Moses* draws on the black church's hermeneutical tradition and promises a communal deliverance from those who oppress God's Children. Hurston's Moses leads his people out of the "Egyptland" of the American South's violent Jim Crow practices and delivers them to a Promised Land that, like her own hometown of Eatonville, Florida, is settled to ensure African-American autonomy.

In his seminal study of African-American literary history, *From Behind the Veil*, Robert Stepto declares that a primary "pregeneric myth"—a shared story or myth that exists within a given culture prior to a literary expression of it but which shapes the culture's

---

[224] Alice Walker, foreword to Robert Hemenway, *Zora Neale Hurston: A Literary Biography*, xviii.

literary forms—undergirds black American literary history: "The primary pregeneric myth for Afro-America is the quest for freedom and literacy."[225] He examines how twentieth-century black writers respond to the earlier "call" of nineteenth-century literary works, such as the slave narratives, to express an eloquent call and response structure in black American literary history. These later authors "revoice" the earlier concerns of their forefathers' quest for literacy. Stepto surely is correct in linking literacy with freedom and determining that literacy is the primary myth which informs the black literary experience, for what is more valuable than learning to decipher the language of a biracial society, most of whose expressions contain not-so-subtle statements of your "proper place" in society?

What Stepto does not consider, however, is the Bible's role in inspiring other African-American pregeneric myths, in general, and in the black quest for literacy, in particular. The Bible was one of the strongest motivations for slaves to learn to read so that they might study "the Book" themselves for messages of hope, looking for passages which said something more than "Servants, obey your masters." Quite simply, slaves were distrustful of white Southern interpretations of the Scriptures and wanted to search the Bible for themselves. Even before these slaves became literate, their inability to read "proved to be less of an obstacle to knowledge of the Bible than might be thought, for biblical stories became part of the oral tradition of the slaves."[226] What they found in their biblical studies, particularly of the Old Testament, were stories of God helping the oppressed, of God aiding His faithful servants. The slaves found the stories of Jonah, Daniel, Elijah, Isaac, and Abraham. However, the story which captured the slaves' imaginations so strongly that it became one of their

---

[225] Robert Stepto, *From Behind the Veil*, ix.
[226] Albert J. Raboteau, *Slave Religion: The "Invisible Institution" in the Antebellum South*, 239, 241.

pregeneric myths was the Exodus story of Moses leading God's children from Egyptian bondage through the Wilderness to the Promised Land. As artists whose childhoods were passed in the black church, Hurston and Wright were very familiar with this story, and its power resonates throughout both *Moses* and *Uncle Tom's Children*. Hurston's novel emphasizes the life lived after deliverance and Wright's collection emphasizes the act of liberating oneself.

In the wake of the recent Hurston revival, critics have been fairly silent regarding *Moses*, focusing much of their attention upon her better known work, *Their Eyes Were Watching God*. Hurston's own writings are also strangely silent regarding *Moses*. Her autobiography, *Dust Tracks On A Road*, was largely written in 1941 and published in 1942, over two years after the publication of *Moses*. In chapter 11, "Books and Things," Hurston provides a brief summary of her writing career, sprinkling it with interesting anecdotes about her work's production, but she fails to even mention *Moses*. Those who have written on *Moses* often focus on its humor. Darwin Turner characterized the novel as an elaborate "joke" which "entertains readers but does not comment significantly on life or people."[227] Much the same point is argued by Robert Hemenway who claims that *Moses* "falls short of its goal" because Hurston "is unable to find a consistent tone that can treat Moses as both divine deliverer and common man"; this supposed inconsistency results because she "seems content with [making] small jokes when a situation calls for tragic irony."[228] What Hemenway and Turner fail to consider are the political implications of laughter. One critic who does understand laughter's liberating effects is John Lowe. In his study of Hurston's humor, *Jump at the Sun: Zora Neale Hurston's Cosmic Comedy*, Lowe

---

[227] Darwin T. Turner, *In a Minor Chord: Three Afro-American Writers and Their Search for Identity*, 111.

[228] Robert Hemenway, *Zora Neale Hurston: A Literary Biography*, 260.

argues that these types of critics have taken too limited a view of "humor's role in discourse, literature, and life."[229] As we have seen, O'Connor's devout Christian beliefs allow her to laugh the laugh of the Redeemed, a superior sort of laugh at the expense of those who struggle with the machinations of Grace. On the contrary, Hurston's *Moses* demonstrates a politically liberating laugh (to paraphrase Ralph Ellison) by slipping the yoke of Jim Crowism through the act of changing the joke the white South told at African-Americans' expense. The Bible not only says "Servants, obey your masters" as the white South preached, but it also gives hope to dispossessed Southern blacks. When critics of Hurston's work sometimes do credit her with a politics of dissent, this most often occurs when reading *Their Eyes Were Watching God*. For instance, in "The Politics of Zora Neale Hurston," David Headon finds evidence of a type of liberation politics in Hurston's work from the 1930s, relying heavily upon a reading of *Their Eyes* which sees Janie as liberating herself from a series of repressive men.[230]

Moses, a novel employing the familiar folk preaching technique of equating Southern black history with the Hebrew exodus from slavery, is conspicuously absent from discussions of liberation politics. Yet, what is more "political" than rewriting one of the key texts the white South used to justify its Jim Crow policies? Whereas an over-emphasis upon salvational concerns within O'Connor's *Wise Blood* deflects attention away from matters of racial prejudice, or an over-emphasis upon the Marxist overtones of Wright's *Uncle Tom's Children* might overlook that text's indebtedness to the black church, the rhetorical move of viewing Hurston as an artist outside of the context of the Jim Crow South closes off discussion of the political implications of her work.

---

[229] John Lowe, *Jump at the Sun: Zora Neale Hurston's Cosmic Comedy*, 211.

[230] David Headon, "The Politics of Zora Neale Hurston," 33.

In *Moses*, Hurston intertextually evokes distinctly black biblical interpretations thereby validating an African-American reading strategy for the Bible—certainly a radical venture. Her vehement efforts to endorse this distinctly African-American cosmogony functions as a type of protest. Walker seems to recognize this, but like most of Hurston's critics, gives with one hand while taking with the other. For instance, while probably doing more to resurrect Hurston's career than anyone else through her thoughtful and sensitive readings of these rediscovered works, bestowing upon Hurston the title of "cultural revolutionary"—a phrase which perfectly embodies *Moses*'s author—Walker stops short of realizing the political significance of Hurston rescuing a black legacy. Referring to comments such as "slavery is the price I paid for civilization," Walker dismisses Hurston's politics as "weird" without even considering the political implications of works such as *Moses*. Walker states in her dedication to the Hurston reader, *I Love Myself When I'm Laughing*, "I think we are better off if we think of Zora Neale Hurston as an artist, period—rather than as the artist/politician most black writers have been required to be."[231] This rhetorical move closes off discussion of the political implications of Hurston's work. Elsewhere in her dedication, Walker seems strangely naïve both to the political connotations of her own analysis when making statements such as "there is enough self-love in [*Their Eyes*]—love of community, culture, traditions—to restore a world. Or create a new one"[232] and to her own sometimes strident position as a black "artist/politician." June Jordan, who first read Hurston at the prompting of Walker, however, recognizes that the "affirmation of Black values and lifestyles within the American context is, indeed, an act of protest. Therefore, Hurston's affirmative work is

---

[231] Alice Walker, *I Love Myself When I'm Laughing*, 3.
[232] Ibid, 2.

profoundly defiant...."[233] With this insight held before us, *Moses* serves as a great call for an African-American leader to unify his or her people into a true community. One study which has recently investigated the powerful political implications of all of Hurston's work is Deborah G. Plant's *"Every Tub Must Sit on Its Own Bottom": The Philosophy and Politics of Zora Neale Hurston.* Plant recognizes that the primary objective of *Moses* is the transformation of a "people's suffering from a potentially disabling experience to an empowering one."[234] This political transformation is accomplished by signifying upon the white South's iconic text, the Bible.

In *The Signifyin(g) Monkey*, Henry Louis Gates posits a theory of intertextuality manifested in many areas of African-American culture. African-American creativity, according to Gates, is informed by borrowing from both black and white traditions. Yet what these artists borrow is not passively or uncritically taken. Using the example of black literary artists, Gates argues that "black writers...learn to write by reading literature, especially the canonical texts of the Western tradition.... But black formal repetition always repeats with a difference."[235] This creating, constructing "difference" is also readily detectable in the history of the black church in America, in both its struggle for autonomy and its teachings. In the words of Theophus Smith, "[w]e may describe the iconic dimension of African American spirituality as a tradition of enactive interpretations or performances; the tradition features, preeminently, interpretive appropriations of *religious* figures and biblical narratives."[236] While under the auspices of

---

[233] June Jordan, "Notes Toward a Black Balancing of Love and Hatred," 87.

[234] Deborah G. Plant, *"Every Tub Must Sit on Its Own Bottom": The Philosophy and Politics of Zora Neale Hurston*, 142.

[235] Henry Louis Gates, Jr, *The Signifyin(g) Monkey*, xxii.

[236] Theophus Smith, *Conjuring Culture: Biblical Formations of Black America*, 134.

white denominational control before the Civil War and as independent bodies of believers after the War, the black church differentiated itself from white Southern Protestants. The black church often emphasized a theology grounded in social justice while the white South remained committed to the theological concerns of personal piety. These are, of course, general tendencies and not hard and fast categorizations. As a Christian church, the black church did address matters of salvation and personal piety, delivering sermons on sex, drinking, card-playing, sometimes sounding much like its white counter-part. The white church took stands on some social issues, particularly on the temperance question. But the general tendencies still stand — the black church concerned itself with social justice and the white church with personal salvation.[237] As Hurston herself reminds us, "while he lives and moves in the midst of a white civilization, everything that [the African-American] touches is re-interpreted for his own use. He has modified the language...and most certainly the religion of his new country."[238]

Specifically, one of the "modifications" Hurston undertakes in *Moses* are alterations in the stories told by the white racist interpretive communities. These white Bible readers underscored passages which they often returned to in order to justify Africans' enslavement. As we have seen, Faulkner's *Light in August* attacks one of the racist interpretive community's legacies, specifically the myth of Ham as a justification for white Southern segregation and violence toward blacks. However, there were many such biblically based prejudices. Southerners often cited the Old Testament stories of patriarchal figures such as Abraham and Isaac who owned slaves, the curse of Cain (where God supposedly put His

---

[237] See William B. McClain's essay, "Free Style and a Closer Relationship to Life," for a similar characterization of the differences between the South's black and white churches.

[238] Zora Neale Hurston, *The Sanctified Church*, 43.

mark on Cain by blackening his skin), the curse of Ham, the lack of a condemnation of slavery by Christ, and the writings of Paul as justifications for their enslavement of blacks.[239] In a text so large and heterogeneous as the Bible, what was often over-looked by white Southern apologists were the passages which directly contradicted such biblical supports for slavery. For example, Deuteronomy 23:15-16 proclaims that "Thou shalt not deliver unto his master the servant which is escaped from his master unto thee: He shall dwell with thee, even among you, in that place which he shall choose in one of thy gates, where it liketh him best: thou shalt not oppress him." Should one own human beings and admonish these slaves to be subservient, or should one give aid and comfort to escaping slaves, thereby invalidating the entire institution of human bondage? There was, of course, only one answer to this question for the white South. However, this ability to read selectively in creating a biblical hermeneutic also worked to the black church's advantage. African-Americans were also empowered by the Protestant imperative to search the Scriptures, and they emphasized those biblical passages speaking of their eventual liberation.

Hurston was fully aware of white Southerners' racist hermeneutical strategies. In fact, she directly confronted one of the South's most pervasive and insidious religious justifications for racism in a one-act play, "The First One," which appeared in Charles S. Johnson's 1927 anthology, *Ebony and Topaz*. "The First One" dramatizes one of the cornerstones of white southern racism, namely Noah's curse upon Ham.[240] Hurston appropriates and

---

[239] See Forrest G. Wood's *Arrogance of Faith* for a discussion of many of the most prevalent biblical defenses of slavery found in the antebellum South.

[240] See the Harper Perennial reprint of *Dust Tracks on a Road*, edited by Henry Louis Gates, Jr, which contains an alternative version of "My People," a chapter from Hurston's autobiography, for another of Hurston's investigations into the myth of Ham.

rewrites a biblical story to critique the white South's racially biased religiosity just as she will to a much greater degree a dozen years later in *Moses*. Hurston's Ham displays all the stereotypical characteristics that Southern whites believed to be inherent in blacks: Ham offers no material sacrifice to Jehovah but plays the happy minstrel, bringing music and dance instead. While Shem and Japheth toil in the fields and with the flocks, Ham entertains the benevolent father (who sounds at times like the kindly plantation owner of antebellum Southern fiction) with songs. Later Noah is duped into cursing whoever has laughed at his drunken nakedness without realizing who is to be the recipient of his anger. Still drunk, Noah bellows, "He shall be accursed. His skin shall be black! Black as the nights, when the waters brooded over the Earth!... Black! He and his seed forever. He shall serve his brothers and they shall rule over him."[241] The amazing thing about "The First One" is that it is essentially a comedy, a spoof of white biblical justifications for racism. At the play's conclusion when Noah banishes Ham and his family, in typical Zora Neale Hurston fashion, they display no anger, no resentment over being black; like his literary creator, this Ham is not "tragically colored." One can easily detect in Ham the same feelings that Hurston expressed in her infamous essay, "How It Feels to Be Colored Me": "There is no great sorrow dammed up in my soul, nor lurking behind my eyes. I do not mind at all. I do not belong to the sobbing school of Negrohood who hold that nature somehow has given them a lowdown dirty deal and whose feelings are all hurt about it."[242] In fact, "The First One" concludes as Ham scorns those he is leaving because he is going to continue laughing, dancing, and singing in the sun.

---

[241] Zora Neale Hurston, "The First One," in *Ebony and Topaz: A Collectaena*, 55.

[242] Zora Neale Hurston, "How It Feels to Be Colored Me," in *The Norton Anthology of American Literature*, 3rd ed., 2:1652.

If the "white Bible" that Hurston attacks in her one-act play and in *Moses* speaks of submission, then the "black Bible" tells the story of Moses and other Old Testament deliverers of God's Chosen People in large, bold letters. Stories of Moses, Daniel, Joseph, and numerous other Hebrew patriarchs provided Southern blacks with an assurance that God delivered the enslaved and punished oppressors in *this* world and not the next. The spirituals provided African-Americans with the artistic medium to express these hopes, and images of these Old Testament heroes are ubiquitous in the black religious cosmogony. In the black community's "communal re-creation" of the deliverance theme, slaves even depicted Jesus as a sort of Old Testament "warrior" fighting for their freedom.[243] Lawrence Levine, in *Black Culture, Black Consciousness*, cites the slaves' transformation of Jesus from Redeemer to Deliverer to support his belief, like Albert J. Raboteau's, in a black biblical hermeneutical practice that selected relevant passages and images from the Bible to construct a message of hope: "This transformation of Jesus is symptomatic of the slaves' selectivity in choosing those parts of the Bible which were to serve as the basis of their religious consciousness."[244] The white South culled through the Bible to find justifications for its racial policies and the black church responded by appropriating that same tool. African-Americans combated racism with the same Bible that the white South used to justify its discriminatory practices.

The strongest identification with and greatest attachment to an Old Testament story was reserved for Moses' delivery of the Children of Israel from Egyptian bondage. The Exodus story exerted a powerful influence over the African-American imagination because the black church "stressed the parallel

---

[243] Lawrence Levine, *Black Culture, Black Consciousness: Afro-American Thought From Slavery to Freedom*, 43
[244] Ibid

between God's directing Moses to lead the Jews out of their bondage and the surety that He would see that they were delivered from enslavement."[245] The common dilemma of enslavement in a foreign land far from their native home, forced by demanding masters to work under cruel circumstances, to "make bricks without straw" — all of these factors encouraged a close identification between African-Americans and a race designating themselves as "God's Chosen People." As Albert Raboteau argues, before and after Emancipation, Southern blacks incorporated "as part of *their* mythic past the Old Testament exodus of Israel out of slavery.... [They] applied the Exodus story, whose end they knew, to their own experience of slavery, which had not ended. In identifying with the Exodus story, they created meaning and purpose out of the chaotic and senseless experience of slavery.... The sacred history of God's liberation of his people would be or was being repeated in the American South."[246] While the black church was still very much Christ-centered and emphasized Jesus as the forgiver of sins, Moses played a pivotal role in the African-American cosmogony because his story "provide[d] a historical example for modern application."[247] Unlike the white church, which often emphasized matters like biblical inerrancy and personal piety, the black church and its ministers presented a Bible punctuated with messages of hope and liberation in order to bolster and edify their congregations. William B. McClain, in his essay, "Free Style and a Closer Relationship to Life," characterizes the differences between the South's black and white Protestant churches: "Preaching in white churches tends to be of a more pastoral nature, emphasizing individuals and their personal behavior rather than the

---

[245] William T. Montgomery, *Under Their Own Vine and Fig Tree: The African-American Church in the South, 1865-1900*, 337.

[246] Raboteau, *Slave Religion*, 311.

[247] Eugene Genovese, *Roll, Jordan, Roll: The World the Slaves Made*, 242.

revolutionary ethic of Jesus and the prophetic judgement on the whole community."[248] Ministers in the black church presented "fiery glad" messages of hope to their congregations.[249] One has to look no further than the religiously inspired rebellions of Denmark Vesey and Nat Turner to find very clear evidence of the "double-edged sword"[250] that African-Americans inherited in adopting and adapting Protestant Christianity.

From her earliest childhood, young Zora Neale Hurston was initiated into and edified by this religious community and quickly mastered its biblical hermeneutic. Her father was a Baptist minister in Eatonville, was invited to preach throughout Florida, and served as moderator for the South Florida Baptist Association.[251] Hurston began early in her reading life to study the Bible, particularly the Old Testament, recognizing it as *the* African-American text of political deliverance. In a classic demonstration of the black church's biblical hermeneutic, Hurston returned again and again to those stories that speak of God's very direct intervention into human affairs. Even as an adult, Hurston declared, "Except for the beautiful language of Luke and Paul, the New Testament still plays a poor second to the Old Testament for me. The Jews had a God who laid about Him when they needed Him." A particularly favorite Old Testament figure was David, a man who was quick to "smite" his people's enemies who were "crying out for a good killing."[252] The Old Testament stories allowed the black church to believe in a God who dispenses retribution, both in this world and the next, upon those who oppress His faithful believers.

---

[248] William B. McClain, "Free Style and a Closer Relationship to Life," 5.

[249] Henry Mitchell, "Two Streams of Tradition," 50.

[250] Raboteau, *Slave Religion*, 290.

[251] Hemenway, *Hurston: A Literary Biography*, 14.

[252] Zora Neale Hurston, *Dust Tracks on a Road*, 40.

The black church was vital to African-American psychological and spiritual health because it proved to be an effective weapon against the white South's racism. Of course, not all white Southern Christians held vitriolic race prejudices. As Eugene Genovese demonstrates, examples of sincere white Christian concern for Africans as human beings and believers can be found in all periods of African-Americans' history.[253] However, the South's major Protestant sects were committed to the "dogma of Negro inferiority, and who thus maintained that the system of black-white separatism represented the normal development of a divinely implanted instinct."[254] This common ideal, so widely held by white congregations, was evident to Hurston. In fact, this doctrine helps shape her characterization of Arvay Henson, the white heroine of her final published novel, *Seraph on the Suwanee*. Arvay attends an unnamed Protestant church which loudly preaches the Southern homily of "Christ and Him Crucified." The minister trumpets racist doctrines from the pulpit, and Arvay learns to scorn a woman who has married a husband considered not "quite white." As in *Light in August* when Joe Christmas first arrives in Jefferson, this man becomes socially feared and stigmatized because his alien status prevents a definite knowledge of his racial history. In Arvay's mind, "the woman had gone back on her kind and *fallen from grace*"[255] (emphasis added) because this woman may have violated the South's prohibition on race mixing. A racism endorsed by white pulpits prevailed across the South declaring that God had "elected" blacks to an inferior status.

Although she was "born with God in the house" and quickly "tumbled right into the Missionary Baptist Church,"[256] Hurston's

---

[253] Genovese, *Roll, Jordan, Roll*, 190.

[254] H. Shelton Smith, *In His Image, But...: Racism in Southern Religion, 1780-1910*, 304-305.

[255] Zora Neale Hurston, *Seraph on the Suwanee*, 242, 120.

[256] Hurston, *Dust Tracks on a Road*, 193.

early religious training left what she called a "lack"[257] in her mind. As an adult, Hurston maintained that "organized creeds are collections of words around a wish."[258] Despite her individual lack of personal faith in organized religion, Hurston treated all religious views with respect, including Christianity and belief systems often dismissed or denigrated from Western cultural biases such as voodoo or folk beliefs. Hurston adamantly believed "that any religion that satisfied the individual urge is valid for that person."[259] This sensitivity to and respect for others' religious beliefs, along with her anthropologist's curiosity, led Hurston to recognize the cultural importance of the loose cluster of associated folk religious beliefs common to Southern blacks.

Hurston stressed the importance of mythic and folkloric stories for Southern blacks. She emphasized both their ability to evolve and their necessity as a foundation for a community that could deliver an antidote to the poisonous influence of slavery and then Jim Crow. In her essay, "High John de Conquer," she demonstrates both folklore's edifying nature and its mutability. Hurston identifies "High John" as one of the central characters of black folklore, dating him all the way back to slavery, yet very few whites have ever heard of him. She explains that during slavery "Old Massa met our hope-bringer all right, but when Old Massa met him, he was not going by his right name. He was traveling, and touristing around the plantations as the laugh-provoking Brer Rabbit."[260] Because folklore stories function as "ceaseless variations upon a theme,"[261] African-American struggles for freedom could be described by High John's exploits in one story, Brer Rabbit's in the next, and some other trickster's in yet another hope-bringing story. It is precisely this ability to shift names and

---

257 Ibid, 194.
258 Ibid, 202.
259 Hurston, *Dust Tracks on a Road*, 193-203, 40, 149.
260 Hurston, *The Sanctified Church*, 70.
261 Zora Neale Hurston, "Characteristics of Negro Expression," 229.

shapes that makes High John so effective as a "hope-bringer."
Regardless of his incarnation—High John, Brer Rabbit, or even
Moses—the liberating hero is always spreading a message of
promise. In Hurston's estimation, these stories serve a religious
function; like the adoption of Old Testament heroes, these folk
stories and folk beliefs help African-Americans to "make a way
out of no way," to survive the American South's violence with
emotional and spiritual health intact. The sacred black world view
is composed of both Protestant doctrine and folk beliefs and
creates a distinctly African-American religiosity that provides an
alternative to white Southern Protestantism's oppression, an
alternative that kept their "legal slavery from becoming a spiritual
slavery."[262]

Hurston once wrote that "Negro folklore is not a thing of the
past. It is still in the making,"[263] and *Moses, Man of the Mountain* is
her best demonstration of this principle. While she was a great
collector of African-American folklore, this novel demonstrates
her participation in the construction of the constantly evolving
mosaic of African-American folklore. Into *Moses,* Hurston
interjects the two crucial elements of the black belief system that
have their roots in the slavery era: the formal creeds of Protestant
Christianity and the more protean beliefs of folk religion. Levine
explains the contribution of each to the construction of black
Southern religiosity.

> Christianity…provid[ed] the assurance of the ephemeral quality
> of the present situation and the glories and retributions to come,
> both in this world and the next, by solidifying the slaves' sense of
> communality, and by reinforcing their feelings of self-worth and
> dignity. Folk beliefs…offered the slaves sources of power and

---

[262] Levine, *Black Culture and Black Consciousness,* 80.
[263] Hurston, "Characteristics of Negro Expression," 229.

knowledge alternative to those existing within the world of the master class.[264]

Rather than accepting wholesale the master class's Christian teachings, slaves engaged in an act of "communal re-creation,"[265] complementing their recently adopted Protestant theology with folk beliefs to create a world view affirming the value of their community.[266] *Moses* capitalizes upon both these folk and Protestant beliefs, transmuting the biblical patriarch into the greatest hoodoo man in the African and African-American traditions. Like High John and other folkloric figures, Hurston's Moses is first and foremost a "hope-bringer" for Southern blacks in their struggle for a better life than that offered by Jim Crow.

To be a true hope-bringer in the long line of such folklore figures for Southern blacks, Hurston's Moses must possess some virtue or endowment that makes him larger than life, that imbues him with the capacity to deliver his message of promise. Moses' gift is his hoodoo or conjuring powers. In his biography of Hurston, Hemenway offers an insightful definition of this belief system: "Hoodoo and conjure are collective terms for all the traditional beliefs in black culture centering around a votary's confidence in the power of a conjure, root, two-head, or hoodoo doctor to alter with magical powers a situation that seems rationally irremediable. At its most basic level it is sympathetic

---

[264] Levine, *Black Culture and Black Consciousness*, 63.

[265] Ibid, 29.

[266] See C. Eric Lincoln's essay "The Black Heritage in Religion in the South" for a similar observation. Lincoln writes: "The black denominations had adopted wholesale the credal confessions and the governing and ritual formats of their white counterparts, *except for those necessary changes giving recognition to the full sovereignty of black churches and the full humanity and responsibility of black people.*" Crucial to making those "necessary changes" were folk beliefs and practices and "vestigial African ritual traditions like the 'ring dance'" (52-53 [emphasis added]).

magic; at its most complex, a highly complicated religion."[267] Practitioners of these arts have fulfilled a vital role in Southern black folk culture since before the Civil War and on into the twentieth century. When bold assertions of civil and social equality by black men and women could lead to death by white mobs, conjuring still fulfilled the vital role of providing an alternative means of responding to and interacting with an often malevolent world, providing "an access to power for a powerless people."[268]

Hurston's Moses explores the secrets of conjuring from his earliest childhood in the Pharaoh's palace. He frequents the palace's libraries and asks the priests how they perform their magic. Mentu (Hurston's pun on the word "mentor"), Moses' servant and attendant to the royal stable, provides the prince's first lessons outside the official ways of seeing and doing sanctioned by the Pharaoh's power structures. Mentu initiates young Moses into the world of black folk belief: he tells "hope-bringing" animal stories, particularly ones about monkeys, and tales of the world's creation. Mentu reveals a world without divisions between the sacred and the secular, where every story teaches to the initiate his moral responsibility to his fellow man. Mentu tells a story of a crippled old lizard that clearly imparts his own needs for companionship and food, so Moses quickly begins to feed his friend from the royal kitchen.[269] One of young Moses' earliest lessons is thus also one of the primary lessons of African-American folklore: cunning, manipulation, and a little love often achieve what force or direct appeals cannot. The old man no longer fights the other palace servants for the morsels left on a pig's cast-off head because his management of Moses ensures that

---

[267] Hemenway, *Hurston: A Literary Biography*, 118-19.
[268] Ibid, 119.
[269] Zora Neale Hurston, *Moses, Man of the Mountain*, 59.

he eats "further back on the hog now."[270] The analogy is clear — to deliver his people from captivity in the Egyptland of the American South, Moses must possess an alternate vision to the dominant culture he opposes.

Mentu's instructions have larger implications for Hurston's analogy of the conditions of the ancient Israelites and Southern blacks. Although Mentu is not himself a Hebrew,[271] his subservient position within the Egyptian social order closely links him on a narrative level with the Israelites. This common status of both Mentu and the Israelites as second-class citizens reveals the generative and transforming power of folklore to ensure psychic health. By this I mean, Moses — conjurer, deliverer, man of power and action — is as much created as appropriated in black Southern folklore. He is obviously taken from the Hebrew Bible and Christian Old Testament, but that is simply his origin. The value of Hurston's Moses is that he is of the folk. Here Hurston alters the biblical story and depicts Moses as a member of the royal house of Pharaoh. Hurston's Moses "consents"[272] to being a Hebrew. Despite his noble lineage, his association with the lowly Mentu and his advocacy of the Hebrews aligns Moses with the oppressed. To be a true hope-bringer, he must have strong ties with the community he seeks to aid while still having the capacity to draw upon resources, knowledge, or power transcending the powerlessness of those he has come to liberate.

The Hebrews of *Moses* are, indeed, a people without hope when Hurston's novel opens; they have no gods to worship, no deities to protect them. On the contrary, Southern white Protestantism adamantly proclaimed that the Hebrews faithfully worshipped Jehovah during their Egyptian enslavement. White Southern Protestants asserted this uninterrupted fidelity to God to

---

[270] Ibid, 61.
[271] Ibid, 71.
[272] Lowe, *Jump at the Sun*, 211.

depict themselves as the ultimate manifestation of God's church on Earth.[273] The white South read the Exodus story typologically as an Old Testament prefiguration of enslavement to sin and the spiritual liberation afforded by Christ's sacrificial death. A tradition of uninterrupted worship of Jehovah, however, did not square with the Africans' experience in America. Just as white slavers sought to deprive Africans of their ancestral histories, language, and religious practices, Hurston's Egyptians strip their slaves of any former religious legacy to break their wills and make them more tractable workers. Jethro describes to Moses the enslaved Hebrews' desperation "down there in Egypt without no god of their own" as having "no more protection than a bareheaded mule."[274]

Jethro will later coach Moses for his role as hope-bringer, but first Moses performs two decisive acts releasing him from his ties to the royal house of Egypt. He kills an Egyptian overseer and then crosses the Red Sea as he flees his angry uncle. The writer/redactor of Exodus renders Moses' killing of the Egyptian in a very laconic style. In the Old Testament account, Moses "spied an Egyptian smiting an Hebrew, one of his brethren. And he looked this way and that way, and when he saw that there was no man, he slew the Egyptian, and hid him in the sand."[275] The biblical account gives no identification of the Egyptian, revealing nothing personal about this man and, certainly, nothing about his social status. In contrast, Hurston's account describes the dead Egyptian with several key terms. Moses' victim is described

---

[273] For example, the Landmark Baptist denomination reached the zenith of its appeal in the first few decades of the twentieth century Landmark Baptists maintained that they could trace a continuous history back to the earliest Christian church of the first century and that they, not Catholicism, represented the one, true church.

[274] *Moses, Man of the Mountain*, 156.

[275] Exodus 2:11-12.

variously as a "foreman,"[276] a "bossman,"[277] and, most significantly, an "overseer."[278] Each of these descriptors underscores that
Moses has just struck a liberating blow for his newly adopted
people. Moses has just fulfilled many of the Southern blacks' silent
wishes, the secret desires of an oppressed people who felt the
overseer's lash on Southern plantations before the Civil War, and
who often worked for cruel bosses and foremen after
Emancipation. Moses has now forged an unbreakable bond with
the Hebrews.

The second of Moses' liberating actions, crossing the Red Sea,
not only foreshadows his upcoming crossing with the newly freed
Hebrews but also emphasizes his new role as an emancipator.
Hurston closes chapter 10 with Moses' renunciation of his former
way of life.

Moses had crossed over. He was not in Egypt. He had crossed
over and now he was not an Egyptian. He had crossed over.... He
did not have friends to sustain him. He had crossed over. He did
not have enemies to strain against his strength and power. He had
crossed over. He was subject to no law except the laws of tooth
and talon. He had crossed over. The sun who was his friend and
ancestor in Egypt was arrogant and bitter in Asia. He had crossed
over. He felt as empty as a post hole *for he was none of the things he
once had been*. He was a man sitting on a rock. He had crossed over
(emphasis added).[279]

Hurston herself achieves the eloquence of a folk preacher with
her measured cadences and repetition of "crossed over." If Moses
is to liberate his newly befriended people, he must first liberate
himself from his former lifestyle, a lifestyle of ease and opulence
that would hinder his identification with the Hebrews. This

---

[276] *Moses, Man of the Mountain*, 93.
[277] Ibid, 94.
[278] Ibid, 95.
[279] Ibid, 103-104.

"crossing" is vital to *Moses* because it allows the young prince to work on behalf of an oppressed people, and the term resonates with theological implications for African-Americans. Just as black preachers urged their congregations to "cross over" into a new life by accepting Jesus Christ, Hurston's Moses will have a similarly liberating effect when he leads the Israelites in "crossing over" from their old life of exploitation and oppression into a new life of freedom.[280] Whereas O'Connor's Hazel Motes yearns for personal salvation, Hurston's Moses struggles for political liberation, to deliver African-Americans into a new life apart from the degradations of living Jim Crow.

Although Hurston's Moses has distanced himself from Egypt's royal house, he still has no direction or mission after crossing the Red Sea. Eventually his wanderings lead him to Jethro who further instructs Moses about conjuring and the ways of Jehovah. While living with and learning from Jethro, both elements of Moses' power—his conjuring and his selection by God—are bestowed upon him in fateful encounters. His hoodoo powers result from his successful quest for the mythical Book of Koptos, and his divine power follows his encounter with the great I AM at the burning bush. In a journey typical of many folk heroes' adventures, Moses seeks great wisdom from a book which is guarded by a frightening monster at the bottom of a body of water. After besting the priest at Koptos in a magic contest, Moses compels them to work for him in the retrieval of the sacred book.

---

[280] Robert Hemenway, in his biography of Hurston, makes a similar argument in reading this passage: "Like a black minister exhorting his congregation to cross over into a *new* life *in* Christ, Hurston's prose not only uses the phrases, but also captures the repetitive pattern and rhythm of the folk sermon—leaving one to gasp for breath and interject the rhythmic *aaaah* of the black preacher after each 'he crossed over'" (*Hurston: A Literary Biography*, 270).

[281] After reading the book of Koptos, Moses "was able to command the heavens and the earth, the abyss and the mountain, and the sea. He knew the language of the birds of the air, the creatures that people the deep and what the beasts of the wilds all said. He saw the sun and the moon and the stars of the sky as no man had ever seen them before, for a divine power was with him."[282] Moses now possesses the means by which to free the Hebrew people from their slavery; the Book of Koptos furnishes him with the power—his "high hand"—to bring plagues against Pharaoh's house and to protect his adopted people. What Moses still lacks is the commission delivered at the burning bush.

Hurston immediately follows her account of Moses' exploits at Koptos with her rereading of his encounter with Jehovah at the burning bush. The meeting is actually the origin of African-American conjuring. As Hurston explains in *Mules and Men*, "Moses never would have stood before the burning bush, if he had not married Jethro's daughter."[283] This God of the mountain, with the deep voice of "rumbling judgment," augments Moses' considerable power by giving him a rod and sharing his powerful, magical words with him. The Moses of Hurston's novel, the progenitor of all African-American conjuring, uses his powers to liberate the enslaved. As Jehovah tells him, "I want you to go down and tell that Pharaoh I say to let my people go."[284] Now he

---

[281] In *Mules and Men*, Hurston tells of her training under a two-headed doctor named Luke Turner, a man who claimed to be the nephew of Marie Leveau Leveau lived and worked in New Orleans during the mid-1800s and is considered, among the initiated, to have been one of the most powerful practitioners of conjuring. Turner told Hurston a story which may have influenced her creation of Moses's battle with the deathless snake: Leveau's greatest totem was a large snake which served only her until it mysteriously disappeared after Leveau's death. Zora Neale Hurston, *Mules and Men*, 194.

[282] *Moses, Man of the Mountain*, 154.

[283] Hurston, *Mules and Men*, 184.

[284] *Moses, Man of the Mountain*, 162.

has a mission and the means to accomplish it—free the enslaved Hebrews and fashion these people into their own community. Through his encounters with the Book of Koptos and the burning bush, this Moses' accumulation of power is analogous to Southern blacks' struggles. His folk beliefs (i.e. his conjuring skills) both augment and adapt the region's dominant religiosity (the Christianity of the burning bush) so that African-Americans might have the necessary anthropological means for constructing a separate, nurturing community.

Moses' task of constructing a people begins dramatically when he leads the Israelites out of Egypt and drowns Pharaoh and his army in the Red Sea; however, he still has not molded them into a cohesive, communal unit. Moses must now use his hoodoo and divine strength to shape the Hebrews into a unified people as they face a hostile tribe, the Amalekites. Joshua serves as a sort of field general and leads the newly liberated Hebrews to victory, but only through Moses is their victory possible. Aaron and another tribal elder, Hur, aid Moses as he calls upon both sources of his power; they support his arms when he grows weary so that he might manifest the power of his conjuring right hand and the magic rod God gave him in his left. While Moses carries the day with his supernatural powers, this battle with the Amalekites is one in which all of God's people must participate. The building and maintaining of an African-American community will not come without a struggle.

Before the battle with the Amalekites, Moses clearly explains the importance of the upcoming conflict, illustrating his point with a folk tale. After equating the Israelites with a "passel of rabbits," Moses recounts the story of how these harmless creatures decided to drown themselves "because nothing looked up to them and nothing was scared of them":

[J]ust before they got to the river there was a marsh that the rabbits had to cross and while they were crossing it they ran over some frogs and the frogs hopped up crying, 'Quit it! Quit it!' So the rabbits said to one another, 'Those frogs are scared of us. We don't need to kill ourselves no more because something in the world is scared of us. Let's go on back home.'... Now that is just what the Israelites need—a victory. They just come out of slavery where they've been stomped down and trampled on. [285]

The hope-bringer must now provide a victory over the dominant culture he opposes. Hurston recounts the same folk tale in *Mules and Men*. Its example as a sort of autotextuality attests to the story's importance in Hurston's own reading of the text of African-American folklore.

As folklorists and scholars are realizing and as African-Americans have long understood, the rabbit is often the coded substitute for black people in folkloric animal stories. Brer Rabbit and all of his rabbit relatives had to survive in the capriciously cruel world with "a little shit, grit and mother-wit." What made the rabbit such an admirable stand-in for Southern blacks—in fact, what elevated him to the status of "hope-bringer"—was that he survived on native intelligence and resilience, overcoming his physically stronger opponents with quick-thinking. In an environment often filled with lynchings and dire warnings for blacks always to remember their "proper place," it was often difficult to find some other inhabitant of the vicious "forest" of Southern race relations who feared or respected them.

This recounting of the rabbit tale within the *Moses* context has an unmistakably revolutionary quality. In its first incarnation in *Mules and Men* (published in October 1935), the rabbit tale is just one of many "lies" told to pass the time on the way to a fishing-hole. Despite the idyllic surroundings of story's first telling, this

---

[285] Ibid, 256.

folk-tale expresses a truth about Southern black political powerlessness. No matter how pleasant life may seem for the moment, the violent caprices of the white South might destroy life's calm exterior. In other words, the rabbits' victory is not yet accomplished in *Mules and Men*. However, *Moses'* "rabbits" (the Israelites) have undergone a profound change. After the battle, Moses and his people stand victorious upon "a truly bloody battle-ground"[286] and are, by virtue of their victory, no longer even rabbits. Moses realizes that he has brought a people, a true community, "out from under Pharaoh with a high hand," "crossed the sea on dry land" with them, and together they "have fought and conquered a nation today."[287] In this rereading of her own work, Hurston's folk tale, collected during her field excursions through the South in 1927-1928, undergoes a revolutionary metamorphosis. Under the beneficent protection of their distinct religiosity, African-Americans have won the hard-fought victory allowing them to exist and pursue their dreams as something other than "rabbits." The deadly seriousness of the Hebrew/ liberated African-Americans' accomplishment and the consequences if they had lost belie previous critics' characterizations of *Moses* as one big joke.

A militant element also manifests itself when Moses dispatches his former allies — Aaron and Miriam who believe themselves to be Moses' siblings — in freeing the Hebrews. For instance, the Israelites often stray, temporarily abandoning the folk religiosity that won them victories over adversaries like the Amalekites. In fact, the recalcitrant Hebrews' apostasy often leads them right back to the Egyptians' religion as when they revert to worshipping Apis, the bull-god, while Moses ascends Mt. Sinai to retrieve the stone tablets containing Jehovah's laws. Hurston lays the blame for most of the newly-freed Israelites' waywardness on

---

[286] Ibid, 259.
[287] Ibid, 260.

Miriam and Aaron. Eventually, Moses removes these two mill-stones from around the collective neck of his people so that the Hebrews might finally claim the Promised Land. In a direct contest with Miriam, Moses proves that he is Jehovah's one, true spokesman and punishes her impudence by afflicting her with leprosy for seven days. Leprosy rendered a person "unclean" in ancient Hebrew society, and such victims were ostracized from the community. Likewise, Hurston's message is clear: any person opposing Moses' mission will suffer both physical affliction and communal scorn.

Moses must also deal directly and violently with Aaron. In a startling rereading of the Old Testament, Hurston's Moses actually kills Aaron so the meddlesome chief-priest will no longer interfere with the Hebrews' progress toward the long-sought Promised Land. Numbers 33:38-39 provides the intertextual antecedent for Hurston's revoicing of the biblical narrative. "And Aaron the priest went up into mount Hor at the commandment of the Lord, and died there, in the fortieth year after the children of Israel were come out of the land of Egypt, in the first day of the fifth month. And Aaron was an hundred and twenty and three years old when he died in mount Hor." Hurston's alteration in *Moses* is extreme. Aaron plans to install himself at the center of the nation's religious life once they claim the Promised Land, but Moses cannot tolerate Aaron's duplicity any longer. Moses kills Aaron to affect a type of redemption, a communal redemption. Whereas O'Connor's characters often use violence for Christian redemption, as Haze's killing the "false prophet," Solace Layfield, Hurston's Moses kills Aaron to ensure the community's deliverance to the Promised Land. "The knife descended and Aaron's old limbs crumpled in the dust of the mountain. Moses looked down on him and wept. He remembered so much from way back.... Moses looked down the mountain at tented Israel and shook his head. 'I have made a nation, but at a price.' Then he buried Aaron and marked the place.... Then he picked up the robes and walked firmly down the mountain to where Eleazar waited."[288] There are several implications of Hurston's intertextual revision. Not only must Moses labor for his adoptive people's freedom, but he must also ensure that nothing detracts from the dignity of their struggle. Perhaps even more importantly, Moses must remove, with decisive force, all impediments to his people's inexorable progress. Like the characters of Wright's *Uncle Tom's Children*, Hurston's Moses realizes that violence may be necessary to liberate African-Americans from the repressive strictures imposed by the white South. However, Hurston's fiction is more intent upon protecting against internal divisiveness than in confronting the white South like Wright.

Hurston's intertextual appropriations from the Exodus story and her subsequent rereadings of these narrative antecedents place her squarely in the tradition of the black folk preacher. *Moses* is one "long black song" of signifying upon a favorite preaching text of black ministers. As Faulkner would say, "the writer must write out of his background,... out of what he [or she] knows," and the Moses story had been a part of the African-American folk cosmogony since before the Civil War. In fact, Hurston is guaranteed a sort of cultural resonance when evoking Moses' story because the entire novel invokes "the traditional Sunday morning sermon on Moses that all black people born before 1965 have heard at least once."[289] In his essay, "Some Negroes in the Land of Goshen," Blyden Jackson realized early on that *Moses's*

---

[288] Ibid, 336.

[289] Walker, *I Love Myself When I Am Laughing*, 176. James Weldon Johnson recreated the powerful poetry of the traditional black folk sermon on Moses in his poem, "Let My People Go," contained in his volume *God's Trombones*. One can hardly escape the revolutionary sentiments like the ones that follow: "Listen! — Listen! — / All you sons of Pharaoh./ Who do you think can hold God's people/ When the Lord God himself has said,/ Let my people go?" (52).

dominant, Old Testament imagery clearly marked it as a type of folk sermon.[290] What Jackson does not fully explore, however, is the novel's *political* function as a folk sermon. The black churchgoer with the hermeneutical skills of the folk tradition understands the full revolutionary implications of the Moses sermon he or she hears "because it is between the lines of Scripture that the narratives of insurgence are delivered."[291] Hurston's fictionalized Moses is firmly grounded in this insurrectionist tradition of black folk preaching and is as necessary and heroic as any actual "real-life" African-American hero or heroine. Hurston's hope-bringing Moses revitalizes a folk tradition and summons a new race leader to join other "militant leaders" in African-American history like David Walker, Ida Wells, Frederick Douglass, Sojourner Truth, and the woman who was often called the Moses of her people, Harriet Tubman.[292]

In many ways, the Promised Land which Moses leads his people toward is reminiscent of Hurston's hometown of Eatonville. The Hebrews' first reports on their future homeland come from Joshua, Caleb, and ten other spies sent by Moses into Canaan. While only Joshua and Caleb advocate an immediate attack to take Canaan, all of Israel is overwhelmed by the produce of the fertile land. The spies return with "a bunch of grapes that it took two men to carry and they brought back melons and cucumbers and various fruits and vegetables."[293] This catalogue of food evokes many of Hurston's lush descriptions of Eatonville, a city of bountiful fruit and vegetables and lots of well-stocked fishing holes. While Richard Wright's autobiographical recollec-

---

[290] Blyden Jackson, "Some Negroes in the Land of Goshen," 106.

[291] Hortense J. Spillers, "Moving on Down the Line: Variations on the African-American Sermon," 41.

[292] Ruthe T. Sheffey, "Zora Neale Hurston's *Moses, Man of the Mountain*: A Fictionalized Manifesto of the Imperatives of Black Leadership," 220.

[293] *Moses, Man of the Mountain*, 313.

tions of childhood are filled with accounts of gnawing hunger and random acts of violence against blacks, Hurston's autobiography tells of eating oranges and receiving enchanting books from the occasional white visitor. As depicted in Hurston's writing, Eatonville is a world apart from the brutality of Wright's Mississippi.

Yet Eatonville represents more than just a full stomach to Hurston; the town occupied a central position in her creative imagination. Eatonville was an autonomous black community where one could be whatever one chose, without encountering many of the restrictions of the dominant culture. Hurston opens her autobiography, *Dust Tracks On A Road*, not with her birth or with a family genealogy, but rather with a history of Eatonville. To fully appreciate her work, one must begin to understand her hometown's importance because, as Hurston says herself, "time and place have had their say."[294]

Hurston closes the introduction of *Mules and Men* with the following description of her hometown: "So I rounded Park Lake and came speeding down the straight stretch into Eatonville, the city of five lakes, three croquet courts, three hundred brown skins, three hundred good swimmers, plenty guavas, two schools, and no jail-house."[295] This brief portrait speaks volumes about her belief in an African-American "Promised Land" — a land of natural beauty that nurtures a true community feeding its members not only with abundant natural resources but also with the big ol' lies told on Joe Clarke's porch. However, to create an Eatonville, Hurston's Moses learns a lesson similar to Richard Wright's own Moses-figure from "Fire and Cloud," Dan Taylor: freedom belongs to those strong enough to claim it.

---

[294] Hurston, *Dust Tracks on a Road*, 1.
[295] Hurston, introduction to *Mules and Men*, 4.

CHAPTER FIVE:

"THE REDS ARE IN THE BIBLE ROOM": THE BIBLE AND POLITICAL ACTIVISM IN RICHARD WRIGHT'S *UNCLE TOM'S CHILDREN*

When Israel was in Egyptland,
Let my people go,
Oppressed so hard they could not stand,
Let my people go.
Go down, Moses...
Tell old Pharaoh,
Let my people go.

The genius of these preachers lay in their ability to adapt what
they had learned to the existing needs and circumstances of their
people and to transpose the white man's message of subservient
obedience into a confident awareness that things were not as they
should be, or as they would be.
— C. Eric Lincoln

LIKE ZORA NEALE Hurston, Richard Wright recognized that African-American religiosity provided psychic health for blacks by assuring them that they would not always be oppressed in the

"Egyptland" of the Jim Crow South. He also recognized the black church's radical potential and its ability to equip Southern blacks with an indigenous belief system for hastening and contributing to their own liberation.[296] Realizing the degree to which Wright viewed black folk culture, particularly the black church, as a source of cultural strength helps to facilitate the kind of reconciliation between Hurston and Wright advocated by June Jordan. She argues that "the functions of protest and affirmation are not, ultimately, distinct: ...affirmation of Black values and lifestyles within the American context is, indeed, an act of protest. Therefore, Hurston's affirmative work is profoundly defiant, just as Wright's protest unmistakably asserts our need for an alternative, benign environment."[297] Both artists viewed African-American religiosity as a source of black vitality and as an integral component of their art, Hurston to promote racial solidarity and Wright to help to stir *"Uncle Tom's Children"* to action.

Despite Ralph Ellison's proclamation that Wright "found the facile answers of Marxism before he learned to use literature as a means for discovering the forms of American Negro humanity,"[298] Richard Wright could not help but "discover" the forms of his African-American heritage. Ellison's pronouncement regarding

---

[296] Several critics have touched upon Wright's relationship with and influence from the black church, most often when discussing *Black Boy*. Michel Fabre's biography, *The Unfinished Quest of Richard Wright*, does an outstanding job of detailing Wright's complex relationship with the black church. See also Robert L. Douglas's "Religious Orthodoxy and Skepticism in Richard Wright's *Uncle Tom's Children* and *Native Son*" and Thomas Larson's "A Political Vision of Afro-American Culture: Richard Wright's 'Bright and Morning Star,'" both included in C. James Trotman's *Richard Wright: Myths and Realities*, for two insightful discussions of Wright's indebtedness to African-American religiosity in the creation of his early fiction.

[297] June Jordan, "Notes Toward a Black Balancing of Love and Hatred," 87.

[298] Ralph Ellison, "The World and the Jug," 120.

Wright's involvement with American Communism overlooks his own role within the CPUSA and its allied fronts during the 1930s. This comment probably has as much to do with disagreements between the two authors as with the prevalent anti-Communist attitude of the nation during the Cold War, the period during which this essay was first published. Reviewers and critics have been suspicious of Wright's communist affinities throughout his career, however. Upon the publication of *Uncle Tom's Children*, Zora Neale Hurston wrote in the *Saturday Review of Literature* that Wright's work presented "the picture of the South that the communists have been passing around of late.... Mr. Wright's author's solution, is the solution of the PARTY—state responsibility for everything and individual responsibility for nothing."[299] As Ellison has also said, quoting Heraclitus, "geography is fate."[300] While the first volume of Wright's autobiography, *Black Boy*, does claim "the strange absence of real kindness in Negroes" and the "cultural barrenness of black life,"[301] it also catalogues many of the joys and strengths of that same black life: the Thomas Wolfe-like lists of beautiful sights, sounds, smells, and sensations of Southern black rural life; the lyrical catalogues of black folk beliefs that he recognized as vital to African-American survival in the South; the indomitable will that Wright inherited from his mother; and, perhaps most importantly for Wright as an artist, his imaginative quest through language for insight into his own lived experience.[302] It is important to remember that Wright's "geographic destiny" also included a thorough indoctrination into the black South's religiosity, a fact also documented in *Black Boy* but often overlooked. His initiation into the symbolism of stories

---

[299] Zora Neale Hurston, "Stories of Conflict," 10.

[300] Ralph Ellison, "Remembering Richard Wright," 198.

[301] Richard Wright, *Black Boy: A Record of Childhood and Youth*, 45.

[302] See Robert Stepto's *From Behind the Veil* on the importance of the pursuit of literacy upon Wright's career as detailed in *Black Boy* and in African-American literary history in general.

and the power of verbally constructed images as taught to him in the black church formed a vital part of his literary apprenticeship.

If Zora Neale Hurston was born with "God in the house" and quickly "tumbled" right into the Missionary Baptist church, Wright proved not to be such a willing participant in Southern black religion. Some of the earliest and most intense exposure he had with the black church came in his childhood when his mother's poor health (brought on by a stroke) forced him to live with his maternal grandmother, Margaret Wilson. Grandmother Wilson was a staunch Seventh Day Adventist, and as a member of her household, Wright was forced to attend services with his grandmother and perform daily pieties such as reciting Bible verses before every meal, much as William Faulkner was made to do at his grandfather's breakfast table. During his childhood, Wright grumbled about the numerous church services he was forced to attend with his mother and grandmother, resented the required family prayers and Bible readings, and resisted every attempt made to save his soul.

In *Black Boy*, Wright recalls the sermons he heard in his grandmother's church, a conversion centered gospel

> clogged with images of vast lakes of eternal fire, of seas vanishing, of valleys of dry bones, of the sun burning to ashes, of the moon turning to blood, of stars falling to the earth, of a wooden staff being transformed into a serpent, of voices speaking out of clouds, of men walking upon water, of God riding whirlwinds, of water changing into wine, of the dead rising and living, of the blind seeing, of the lame walking;...a cosmic tale that began before time and ended with the clouds of the sky rolling away at the Second Coming of Christ....[303]

---

[303] Wright, *Black Boy*, 13.

Wright claims in *Black Boy* to have "remained basically unaffected"[304] by the emotional appeals to save his soul made during these colorful sermons of his early childhood, perhaps because he did not want to compromise his narrative persona's carefully cultivated sense of uncompromising independence. The Wright of *Black Boy* is virtually self-created. But, as Michel Fabre notes, Wright was tremendously influenced by these sermons' vivid images and stories,[305] learning early lessons in story-telling and narrative technique and later harkening back to them as he intertextually invokes them in his mature fiction. However, while making this observation, Fabre mentions only "Big Boy Leaves Home" as a noteworthy example of a work from *Uncle Tom's Children* that draws upon Wright's early biblical and religious training at the hands of his Grandmother Wilson.

Wright most clearly and extensively explains his ideas about the radical nature he perceived within the black church in "Blueprint for Negro Writing," an essay originally published in *The New Challenge* in 1937. Written while composing *Uncle Tom's Children* and during the early stages of his relationship with communism, Wright is filled with the ardor of the newly converted in this essay. He shows how his Marxist faith informs his view of the black church's role in the upcoming inevitable revolution. The black communist artist will be in the vanguard of this struggle as if to receive the baton passed on from the black church: "With the gradual decline of the moral authority of the Negro church, and with the increasing irresolution which is paralyzing Negro middle-class leadership, a new role is devolving upon the Negro writer. He is being called upon to do no less than create values by which his race is to struggle, live, and die."[306] Despite his criticism of the black church, Wright does not dismiss

---

[304] Ibid, 124.
[305] Michel Fabre, *The Unfinished Quest of Richard Wright*, 35.
[306] Richard Wright, "Blueprint for Negro Writing," 398-99.

it as having no value in the revolutionary struggle for full participation in American democracy. Elsewhere in this essay, Wright asserts that "there is...a culture of the Negro which is his and has been addressed to him; a culture which has...helped to clarify his consciousness and create emotional attitudes which are *conducive to action*. This culture has stemmed from two sources: 1) the Negro church; 2) and the folklore of the Negro people"[307] (emphasis added).

In Wright's vocabulary, action almost always means collective, political action as in *Uncle Tom's Children*, particularly, "Fire and Cloud." The Reverend Dan Taylor struggles over whether or not he should help the local communist organizers stage a demonstration to petition the city's power brokers for help in feeding the town's poor, both black and white. In this gesture of racial unity, Wright's invocation of the South's response to the Bible sets his intertextual practice apart from Faulkner, Hurston, and O'Connor's. There are no examples of biracial congregations in *Light in August, Moses, Man of the Mountain,* or *Wise Blood.* In *Light in August*, the white character Doc Hines enters into black churches, but he goes only to preach sermons of white superiority; in *Moses*, Moses and the liberated Southern blacks keep to themselves to insure that they will not become victimized again by the Jim Crow South; and in *Wise Blood*, the novel's single black character, a Pullman porter, delivers the worldly-wise message to Hazel that Jesus is long dead. But, when Taylor is finally galvanized into action, he feels a part of a "many-limbed, many-legged, many-handed" and multi-colored organism as he participates in the march. Taylor has discovered a new and deeper relationship with his community and with God through his commitment to social justice. And Wright advocates much the same in "Blueprint for Negro Writing." Folklore and the church have been the African-American's medium for expressing what

---

[307] Ibid, 396.

Wright labeled African-American "racial wisdom" (although "cultural wisdom" might be a more accurate phrase). In turn, this wisdom has given *meaning* to American blacks' experiences and suffering. In Wright's opinion, the black church has done much to crystallize and shape the collective "meaning" of the African-American experience because black religiosity has long served as an "antidote for suffering and denial."[308] The "meaning [of] their suffering" is crucial for producing activism in African-Americans because "at the moment when a people begin to realize a meaning in their suffering, the civilization that engenders that suffering is doomed."[309] To continue Wright's metaphor, if the black church had traditionally functioned as an "antidote" for racial oppression, he believed it was time for it to become politically active in the fight against Jim Crow and to act as a "prevention" against further racial injustices.

James H. Cone has described the black church's theology as a type of "liberation theology."[310] After all, the black church has been about liberation since its earliest beginnings: in its adopting the pregeneric myth of Moses delivering God's children from bondage; in its embracing a biblical hermeneutic grounded in the here and now; in its serving as one of the earliest outlets for black creativity and community advancement, African-American religiosity has served "roles of both protest and relief."[311] Wright's contribution to the cultural conversation on the Bible in the South is outlined in "Blueprint for Negro Writing" and even more forcefully in the stories of *Uncle Tom's Children*. He insists that the

---

[308] Ibid.

[309] Ibid, 396-97.

[310] James H. Cone, "Black Theology as Liberation Theology," 178. The title of Cone's essay is a clear allusion to the work of Latin American theologians such as Gustavo Guttiérrez and other pioneers in the development of liberation theology.

[311] Joseph R. Washington, Jr., "Folk Religion and Negro Congregations: The Fifth Religion," 52.

black church must become even more political and must fully actualize its revolutionary potential to evolve into an even greater agent for dramatic action in righting the social wrongs committed against African-Americans.

Crucial to Wright's involvement with the Communist Party, USA (CPUSA) was the party's endorsement of full civil and equal rights for African-Americans. Yet, Wright detected a flaw in the party's strategy for winning the support of large numbers of African-Americans. For Wright, the CPUSA's emphasis upon enlisting the masses made them too inflexible in meeting the particular demands of the specific people they sought to help. In *American Hunger*, he writes, "The Communists, I felt, had oversimplified the experience of those whom they sought to lead. In their efforts to recruit masses, they had missed the meaning of the lives of the masses, had conceived of people in too abstract a manner." In Wright's opinion, American communism was not responsive enough to black culture, and he saw himself as a mediator between the new dispensation of communism and the vitality and specific needs of African-Americans. Elsewhere in *American Hunger*, Wright expresses the depth of the communist convictions he held during the writing of *Uncle Tom's Children* when he says that "with the exception of the church and its myths and legends, there was no agency in the world so capable of making men feel the earth and the people upon it as the Communist party."[312] Of his mediating role, Wright goes on to say, "I would make voyages, discoveries, explorations with words and try to put some of that meaning back. I would address my words to two groups: I would tell Communists how common people felt, and I would tell common people of the self-sacrifice of Communists who strove for unity among them."[313] Essential to communicating the feelings and hopes of the Southern blacks he

---

[312] Richard Wright, *American Hunger*, 122.
[313] Ibid, 65-66.

knew first-hand and interviewed while writing *Uncle Tom's Children* was Wright's demonstration of the church's principal role in the community — its Bible, its strong, determined congregations, and its devotion to civil equality.

The CPUSA helped Wright insist upon political activism from the black church. In many ways, communism was Wright's church. While he later withdrew from the party and became increasingly outspoken in his opposition to international communism,[314] Wright was a committed member of the party when he wrote *Uncle Tom's Children*. What Wright initially found so appealing about communism was the highly spiritual sense of community it inspired in him. "[M]y attention was caught by the similarity of the experiences of workers in other lands, by the possibility of uniting scattered but kindred people into a whole.... Out of the [communist] magazines I read came a passionate call for the experiences of the disinherited, and there was none of the lame lisping of the missionary in it."[315] He went so far as to use Protestantism's discourse to underscore his youthful commitment to the CPUSA by describing his joining as a "total commitment of faith."[316]

As Cornel West reminds us, "the classical Marxist critique of religion is not an *a priori* philosophical rejection of religion; rather, it is a social analysis of, and historical judgement upon, religious practices."[317] Much the same could be said of Wright's

---

[314] See Paul Gilroy's *The Black Atlantic*, 165-70, for a discussion of Wright's increasing disillusionment with communism, particularly after leaving the United States. See also Cedric Robinson's *Black Marxism* and its discussion of Wright's critique of Marxism (416-40), wherein Robinson quotes Wright as saying, "Marxist ideology...is but a transitory make-shift pending a more accurate diagnosis.... Communism may be but a painful compromise containing a definition of man by sheer default" (433).

[315] Richard Wright, "I Tried To Be A Communist," 118.

[316] Wright, *American Hunger*, 133.

[317] Cornel West, "Religion and the Left," 199.

investigation of the black church in "Blueprint for Negro Writing" as he never faults the church as an institution, but exhorts it toward greater political participation. In "On the History of Early Christianity," Frederick Engels writes: "The history of early Christianity has notable points of resemblance with the modern working-class movement. Like the latter, Christianity was originally a movement of oppressed people: it first appeared as the religion of slaves and emancipated slaves, of poor people deprived of all rights.... Both Christianity and the workers' socialism preach forthcoming salvation from bondage and misery...."[318] In "Blueprint for Negro Writing," Wright credits the black church with being informed by a quest for freedom.[319] Wright explored these similarities and possibilities for tactical alliances between Marxism and Christianity in "Fire and Cloud" and "Bright and Morning Star," the last two stories from *Uncle Tom's Children*. These alliances were not explicitly explored by black theologians and historians until the Black Power Movement of the 1960s and 1970s. Wright celebrates the real-life Moses figures of African-American history—Nat Turner, Harriet Tubman, Sojourner Truth—by creating the Moses-like freedom fighters of "Fire and Cloud" and "Bright and Morning Star."

As Abdul JanMohamed has noted, the cohesion of *Uncle Tom's Children* derives from its incremental repetition of themes,[320] with Wright's concerns progressing outward from individual survival toward community solidarity and eventual political activism. Wright even revised the collection for its subsequent 1940 publication by adding an introductory essay, "The Ethics of Living Jim Crow," and a fifth and concluding story, "Bright and Morning Star," to make this expansion more explicit. Wright explained his

---

[318] Frederick Engels, "On the History of Early Christianity," 316.

[319] Wright, "Blueprint for Negro Writing," 397.

[320] Abdul JanMohamed, "Rehistoricizing Wright: The Psychopolitical Function of Death in *Uncle Tom's Children*," 192.

revision in "How 'Bigger' Was Born," the introduction to *Native Son*. He says, "I had written a book of short stories which was published under the title of *Uncle Tom's Children* [in 1938]. When the reviews of that book began to appear, I realized that I had made an awfully naïve mistake. I found that I had written a book which even bankers' daughters could read and weep over and feel good about."[321] Wright wanted to deprive his readers of the consolation of tears and challenge them with an unmistakably political work in the revised book. Whites were stripped of their stereotypical views of blacks as contented workers and were faced with the unsettling specter of increased CPUSA activity in their region. Blacks were faced with a radical challenge that called upon its strongest cultural institution—the church—to increase its political activities. Wright maintained that "Big Boy Leaves Home" and all of the stories of *Uncle Tom's Children* posed one central question: "What quality of will must a Negro possess to live and die with dignity in a country that denied his humanity?"[322] By the collection's (revised) conclusion, there is no mistaking Wright's answer to this question—African-Americans must use the legacy of the black church, which has always maintained the worth and dignity of its members, but they must employ that spiritual legacy within the collectivization of Marxist politics to press toward the goal of civil equality.

Wright's 1940 version of *Uncle Tom's Children* included the autobiographical introduction, "The Ethics of Living Jim Crow." The essay's focus upon Wright's search for employment in an economic system controlled by whites reinforces the entire collection's demand for a revolutionary opposition to Southern Jim Crowism. As autobiography, the essay establishes the book as a physical object outside of the narrative world and evokes a

---

[321] Richard Wright, "How 'Bigger' Was Born"(introduction to *Native Son*) 31.

[322] Wright, *American Hunger*, 88-89.

historical context—Wright's own life as it was lived in the Jim Crow environment of the racist South.[323] Wright's documentation of the violence and day-to-day humiliations of living Jim Crow exposes the falsity of popular conceptions of Southern tranquility, the propaganda behind songs like the one which serves as the book's epigraph:

> Is it true what they say about Dixie?
> Does the sun really shine all the time?
> Do sweet magnolias blossom at everybody's door,
> Do folks keep eating 'possum, till they can't eat no more?
> Do they laugh, do they love, like they say in ev'ry song?...
> If it's true that's where I belong.

Wright makes it clear that he never knew this Edenic South, that land flowing with milk and honey so reminiscent of Hurston's Eatonville, Florida. Instead, he was confronted with the same racial violence experienced by his literary characters. Unlike most of the characters from *Uncle Tom's Children*, however, Wright would never surrender himself to the black church, despite the powerful pull of its symbols and its "dramatic vision of life."[324]

In "Big Boy Leaves Home," the collection's first story, biblical intertextuality evokes the hopes and dreams of a life lived free from the horrors of Jim Crow. The Bible was revoiced in the black church's spirituals and social structure, sustained the African-American community, and offered shelter from the white South's racist fury, but its use in this story offers no means of successfully overcoming that racism. For instance, as Big Boy and his friends make their way to the fateful water hole on old man Harvey's

---

[323] See C. Vann Woodward's *The Strange Career of Jim Crow* for an account of how the white South gradually enacted Jim Crow legislation throughout the region.

[324] Wright, *Black Boy*, 123.

property, they sing the spiritual "This Train Bound for Glory" about the "freedom train" that they hope will one day deliver them to the Promised Land. Spirituals have always spoken with a double voice, promising heavenly rewards for faithful service to God and deliverance here in this life. The boys sing of these promises when they hear an actual train heading North toward greater freedom than they know in the Jim Crow South. The dual nature of the spirituals is even clearer when the boys hear another north-bound train whistle after they reach the swimming hole. Their speech reinforces the association of the "freedom train" with spiritual *and* social liberty outside of the South:

> Far away a train whistled.
> "There goes number seven!"
> "Headin fer up Noth!"...
> "Lawd, Ahm goin Noth some day."
> "Me too, man."
> "They say colored folks up Noth is got ekual rights."[325]

Their song and speech are vaguely prophetic because the social network of the black church engineers Big Boy's escape after he shoots the white soldier in self defense. Everything about this escape evokes the Underground Railroad which delivered escaped slaves to the North: Big Boy hides in a kiln in the side of the hill where the boys used to play as if they were train conductors, and he escapes in the pre-dawn darkness. A church elder's son is a truck-driver who makes regular deliveries to the North, and Big Boy will hide until morning and catch a ride to Chicago.

In later stories, the church becomes an organ of political action that advances against the South's Jim Crow laws, but it is powerless to stop Bobo's lynching in this story and can only

---

[325] *Uncle Tom's Children*, 27.

provide Big Boy's escape. After the murders of Lester and Buck, Big Boy manages to flee to his house where his parents assemble the church elders to plot his escape; however, this same congregation seems powerless to stop the white mob from burning down Big Boy's parents' house in retribution. Just like when Big Boy squeezes Bobo's neck so that Lester and Buck will abandon their friendly wrestling match, the white South realized that in the absence of a politically unified and active black church "a little heat,"[326] as in a well-timed cabin burning or lynching, will often dissuade others from opposing Jim Crow.

Biblical intertextuality provides ironic commentary in "Down By the Riverside" by contrasting the church's otherworldly promises with the horrors of political disfranchisement and second class citizenship. As neighbors and fellow church-members gather in his house during the Great Mississippi Flood of 1927 to pray for his wife, who is in the throes of child labor, Mann considers the problem of transporting his wife to the hospital in a stolen rowboat. As he sets off rowing against the current of the flooded river and the tide of Southern white racism, the story accelerates with a nightmarish speed. Mann kills the boat's original owner in self defense and delivers his wife to the Red Cross only to find that she died in childbirth. He then confronts the family of the man he killed when he helps to evacuate stranded families in town, and he finally forces the armed soldiers to shoot him when they discover that he killed a white man. Mann stakes everything on his faith in a supernatural deliverance, yet the soldiers and their guns prove to be powerful reminders of the necessity for political action. The refrain of the spiritual sung at Mann's house, "Ah ain gonna study war no mo," is the story's strongest ironic indictment of the militarily enforced Jim Crow system that eventually costs Mann his life. What endows him with the superhuman strength he displays is his faith

---

[326] Ibid, 23.

in God. As he says in one of his interior monologues, "Nobody but God could see him through this.... He would have to trust God and keep on and go through with it, that was all."[327] Mann's prayers for deliverance, however, are answered only with his death. As Abdul JanMohamed argues, death becomes Mann's "only viable, but highly paradoxical, route of escape from [the] radical liminality" of a Jim Crow existence because African-American religiosity offers little hope (in this story, at least) of providing a weapon for fighting against the "social death" of Southern racial oppression.[328]

"Long Black Song," the middle story of *Uncle Tom's Children*, is the fulcrum upon which the collection pivots. Here Wright addresses more explicitly his larger, societal concerns. The New Testament Silas renounces worldly gain to proclaim the early church's gospel with the apostle Paul, but Wright's pursues money and property to the exclusion of everything else. So strong is his commitment to material gain that Silas often neglects Sarah, his wife, and their child. While listening to a spiritual on a gramophone, Sarah succumbs to the advances of the white college-boy salesman who tries to interest her in buying the fancy combination clock and record-player.[329] Silas refuses to accept

---

[327] Ibid, 71.

[328] JanMohamed, "Rehistoricizing Wright," 192.

[329] Some critics maintain that Sarah was raped by the white salesman See, for example, C. James Trotman's introduction to *Richard Wright: Myths and Realities*, entitled, "Our Myths and Wright's Realities" (xii). Sarah initially resists the young man's advances, but her longing for her first lover, Tom, and the memory of the spiritual played on the gramophone combine to produce a sexual ecstasy in her that Wright describes in rapturous tones. See Myles Raymond Hurd's "Between Blackness and Bitonality: Wright's 'Long Black Song'" for a thorough examination of the sexual politics between Sarah and the white salesman. Hurd sees parallels between their encounter at the well and the New Testament story, recounted in John 4:5-19, of Jesus and a Samaritan woman who discuss her infidelity at a well.

what he sees as a betrayal with the easy tolerance demanded by the Jim Crow South. As John Lowe notes, "Like his biblical counterpart, Silas refuses flight, and elects to stay where he is, letting the enemy come to him."[330] In his violent and inarticulate struggle against white racism, Silas bears a strong resemblance to another of Wright's literary characters, Native Son's Bigger Thomas. Both characters are filled with a similar murderous rage and refuse to abide by the pervasive racist mores of their environments. Both grapple with a language inadequate to express their anger and to achieve their greatest eloquence in their violent refusal to tolerate America's color prejudices.

Wright's commentary upon the forces that could produce a Bigger Thomas ring equally true of Silas: the creation of such an individual is, in Wright's opinion, largely attributable to a person's becoming "estranged from the religion and folk culture of his race."[331] Bigger estranges himself from his culture when his desire to be like the glamorous, flickering shadows of the movie screens and his immersion in petty thievery and anger and indignation of ghetto-life. Silas, on the other hand, estranges himself by pursuing material gain in the same ruthless manner as the white landowners. Silas is isolated even in death, unlike the other characters of Uncle Tom's Children who force confrontations with the Jim Crow society such as Dan Taylor from "Fire and Cloud" and Aunt Sue from "Bright and Morning Star." While the Jim Crow system deprived him of his wife and child, Silas temporarily masters oppressive whites with their own weapons, the material emblems of the white South's Jim Crow ideology, i.e., a gun and a whip. Unfortunately, his lynching effects no appreciable change in the political realities of the Jim Crow South. Like Joe Christmas' actions before his death in Light in August, the

---

[330] John Lowe, "Wright Writing Reading: Narrative Strategies in Uncle Tom's Children," 62.

[331] Wright, "How 'Bigger' Was Born," 15.

white South has no glimpse into Silas' decision to become a "hard" man and resist the social system that has taken everything for which he has worked so hard. Also like Christmas, his lynching serves as another buttress and sanction for the white South's racist ideology.

Uncle Tom's Children moves through the stages of African-American responses to the oppressive white South. "Fire and Cloud" is the collection's first story to fully marshal the black church's latent political energy within its religious discourse. The collection explores the elements within African-American religiosity that deflect concerns for social justice and emphasize survival by means of escape ("Big Boy Leaves Home"). Then it moves to those components of the black church that stress heavenly rewards for enduring seemingly inescapable racial tribulations here on earth ("Down By the Riverside"). Next it depicts the ineffectual anger of a man cut off from the social network of the black church by the white South's racist economic and social system ("Long Black Song"). But Dan Taylor is the first character in *Uncle Tom's Children* to reconcile the aims of communism and the black church.

Wright would go on to have his well-documented break with the CPUSA, but his commitment to communism was at its height in the 1930s, the period in which he drafted the stories of *Uncle Tom's Children*, and it was also a period which held great promise for combining the efforts and energies of the black church with the CPUSA, which reached the zenith of its influence in this era. In 1931, the CPUSA provided legal counsel for the defendants in the Scottsboro case, and their advocacy of these young men proved to be a major factor in gaining a sympathetic audience among Southern blacks. As a result of their efforts, the communists succeeded in making the case an international *cause celebre* and gained invitations to speak in many black pulpits.[332] A year after the Scottsboro case the in-roads of the CPUSA (which were extremely hard won considering the rabid anticommunist sentiment of the white South) were reflected in the opinions expressed by participants in a symposium of leading black newspaper editors printed in *The Crisis*. While Roscoe Dunjee expressed skepticism toward but a willingness to listen to radical whites with apparent "love in [their] heart[s]" for Southern blacks, Carl Murphy said that "the Communists appear to be the only party going our way. They are as radical as the NAACP were 20 years ago."[333]

"Fire and Cloud" opens with Reverend Dan Taylor debating what role he should take in resolving a tense stalemate over food distribution during the Depression. Whereas Hurston's intertextual figuration of Moses relies only upon a distinctive African-American religiosity, Taylor struggles to decide if he will support the Party's agenda. Should he endorse the direct action and public demonstration advocated by local communist organizers, Hadley and Green, or should he instruct his congregation to maintain their faith in God's eventual deliverance and not participate in the planned communist march? On one hand, the direct confrontation advocated by Hadley and Green seems to offer hope through the strength possible in their numbers. He thinks that a large, organized assembly "could do *something*, awright! Mabbe ef fiv er six thousan of us marched downtown we could *scare* [the white city administration] inter doin something! Lawd, mabbe them Reds *is* right!"[334]

On the other hand, Taylor still maintains a firm faith in God the Deliverer, the God who liberated His People from Egypt and

---

[332] Harvey Klehr, *The Heyday of American Communism: The Depression Decade*, 335-36.

[333] Roscoe Dunjee and Carl Murphy, "Negro Editors on Communism: A Symposium of the American Negro Press," 154, 147.

[334] *Uncle Tom's Children*, 130.

destroyed Pharaoh for daring to contradict His will. He longs for divine retribution, "The good Lawds gonna clean up this ol worl some day! Hes gonna make a new Heaven n a new Earth! N Hes gonna do it in a eye-twinkle change; Hes gotta do it! Things cant go on like this ferever!"[335] Wright quickly reconciles these two courses of action when he likens Taylor to Moses. Before the Depression's economic hardships and a reduction in land available for black farmers, Taylor had been "like Moses leading his people out of the wilderness into the Promised Land."[336] Invoking Moses assures a hallowed sanctioning of his eventual alliance with Hadley and Green because, like his biblical predecessor, Taylor is working to liberate God's people. Using the figure of Moses suggests a reconciliation of the story's opening dichotomy: Moses is both man of God and man of action, serving Jehovah by liberating his chosen people.

But Moses is not the only biblical character intertextually evoked in this story; Deacon Smith plays both Judas and Satan to Taylor's Christ because, to fulfill a kind of typology within "Fire and Cloud," Taylor must be both Moses and Jesus. Like Christ, Taylor is presented with the temptation to abandon his mission— Jesus refuses the worldly temptations of Satan in the Wilderness, and Taylor politely deflects the mayor's bribe to "take care of him" if he "does the right thing."[337] Following Taylor's rejection of this offer, the mayor sounds suspiciously like Pilate washing his hands of the whole affair when he tells the reverend that compromise is no longer an option. Mayor Bolton says, "Ive done all I could, Dan. You wouldn't follow my advice, now the rest is up to Mister Lowe and Chief Bruden here."[338] Like Christ who was persecuted and bore his tribulations "without a mumblin'

---

335 Ibid, 131.
336 Ibid.
337 Ibid, 151.
338 Ibid, 152.

word" but will, according to the spirituals, implement God's plan of divine justice, the reverend is beginning to realize the necessity of undertaking his own liberating mission. These New Testament evocations suggest parallels between Taylor and the Gospel accounts of Jesus. As James Cone reminds us, associating Christ with liberation is a cornerstone of what he calls "black theology" and is an association that can trace its roots back at least as far as Nat Turner who was inspired by Jesus to "the spirit of violent revolution against the strictures of slavery."[339] Wright's characterization of Taylor fluctuates between these two affiliations, sometimes invoking Moses and sometimes Jesus, but always evoking their emancipating missions. Drawing upon the liberating legacy of these two biblical figures, Taylor adopts the communist's plan and leads the march, synthesizing black political power and the black church.

Taylor's faith in the righteousness of his mission shines through the prayer he offers to comfort some of his church members. Narrative tension is at its height as the preacher juggles the demands of everyone who has crowded into his house to meet with him. He must calm his flock's fears (stirred up by the "snake in the grass," Deacon Smith), deliver a decision to the Party organizers, and pacify the white civic leaders who have come to demand that he not lead the march. Despite this chaos, Taylor takes time to edify the assembled believers and assure them that they play a key role in God's intricate plan. Throughout the call and response format of Taylor's prayer, he invokes numerous examples of God's benevolence, outlining the Bible's course of sacred history from Genesis to Revelation, particularly emphasizing the constancy and fidelity God shows toward His Chosen People. Beginning with the Creation, Taylor lists God's intercessions on behalf of His people—the Exodus out of Egypt, the deliverance of the Hebrews from the fiery furnace, the victory

---

[339] James H. Cone, *God of the Oppressed*, 114.

of the Israelites over their enemies at Jericho. He concludes the prayer with a specific request, asking for direction in guiding his flock: "Speak t our hearts n let us know what Yo will is!... Try us, Lawd, try us n watch us move t yo will!" Just like previous generations of faithful servants, Taylor and his church will comply with God's will once they discern what He would have them do. In contrast, the avaricious white landowners are depicted as violating God's divine plan. If the black church is seeking to serve God, the dominant white South is guilty of controverting God's wishes: "The white folks say we cant raise nothin on Yo earth! They done put the lans of the worl in their pockets! They done fenced em off n nailed em down! Theys a-tryin t take Yo place, Lord!"[340] Underscoring the common concerns of the CPUSA and the black church, Taylor's prayer is issued on behalf of the entire African-American community and indicts greedy whites for attempting to disrupt God's sacramental plan. In his prayer, the doctrines of both Christianity and Marxism assure that everyone should have equal rights. Taylor and, by extension, the black church have turned the tables on Southern whites who appeal to the Bible to characterize African-Americans as sub-human; in this cosmogony, these racist interpretive communities have clearly violated God's promises.

To inscribe Marxist doctrine within the black church and activate what he saw as the revolutionary potential within black religiosity, Wright insists upon a new dispensation. Whereas the white Southern church viewed Christ's sacrificial death as superseding the rituals of the Hebrew Law, the South's Jim Crow oppression of Southern blacks demands a new system of promises. In the Gospels, Jesus states that his intention is to realize the writings of the Hebrew Bible, not to destroy them in any way: "Think not that I am come to destroy the law, or the prophets: I am not come to destroy, but to fulfill. For verily I say unto you,

---

[340] *Uncle Tom's Children*, 138.

Till heaven and earth pass, one jot or one tittle shall in no wise pass from the law, till all be fulfilled."[341] Jesus proclaims himself the fulfillment of the Law, its ultimate, truest expression. In a similar fashion, Wright's fiction maintains that the truest and most politically committed expression of the black church's love and concern for its members can be voiced with the aid of communist doctrine. Wright symbolizes this inscription of the CPUSA's goals into the black church by placing the communists Hadley and Green within the Bible Room. Their political agenda should suffuse the Scriptures. Even though Taylor initially distances himself from the organizers by referring to them as "them Reds," which is the same pejorative label affixed by the white civic leaders, Taylor later calls the communist organizers "Brother Hadley" and "Brother Green." Most notably, Taylor even extends this title of love and respect normally reserved for other Christians to Hadley, a man whose white skin would ordinarily make the reverend view him at least with suspicion, if not outright animosity.

As a result of his refusal to abandon the demonstration, Taylor is kidnapped and tortured by the city council's henchmen, and he undergoes a metaphorical "death and rebirth."[342] As he makes his way home, he must cross through a white neighborhood, which, as Wright reminds us in "The Ethics of Living Jim Crow," was a particularly dangerous situation for a black man in the Jim Crow South.

> Negroes who have lived South know the dread of being caught alone upon the streets in white neighborhoods after the sun has set. In such a simple situation as this the plight of the Negro in America is graphically symbolized. While white strangers may be in these neighborhoods trying to get home, they can pass unmolested. But the color of a Negro's skin makes him easily

---

[341] Matthew 5:17-18.
[342] JanMohamed, "Rehistoricizing Wright," 221.

recognizable, makes him suspect, converts him into a defenseless target.[343]

Caught in this dangerous situation, Taylor views these white houses as emblems of the unjust system he has struggled against. The pain of his beating has transformed Taylor into a "pillar of fire." God directed the Hebrews to follow a pillar of fire out of Egyptian bondage, and Taylor likewise longs to lead his people out of the bondage of the white South's racial injustices. Taylor looks at the white homes and thinks, "Some days theys gonna burn! Some days theys gonna burn in Gawd Awmightys fire!"[344] Filled with a fervent desire to fulfill this prophesy, to render some miraculous service to his people, Taylor pleads, "Gawd, ef yuh gimme the strength Ahll tear this ol buildin down! Tear it down, Lawd! Tear it down like ol Samson tore the temple down!"[345] Like an Old Testament deliverer, Taylor longs to be an instrument of God's divine will, but he desires to fulfill a New Testament-like apocalyptic vision where a new heaven and earth of economic and political equality replaces the reality of the Jim Crow South.[346]

Taylor succeeds in this role of deliverer and leads his people to the Promised Land of political participation. The crowd is conscious of parallels between their struggle for liberation and the

---

[343] Richard Wright, "The Ethics of Living Jim Crow," 10.

[344] *Uncle Tom's Children*, 167.

[345] Ibid.

[346] For a different reading of "Bright and Morning Star," see JanMohamed's "Rehistoricizing Wright: The Psychopolitical Function of Death in Uncle Tom's Children," perhaps the most thorough, sophisticated, and engaging treatment of this collection as a whole. In his essay, JanMohamed argues that "religion becomes the potential source of rebellion, but the final transformation of Taylor does not occur until that source of power is ridiculed and seems to have failed." He goes on to argue that Taylor's prayer during his lynching falls upon deaf ears because of the "void left by God's absence" (222, 223).

struggle of their Old Testament predecessors, singing as they march:

> So the sign of the fire by night
> N the sign of the cloud by day
> A-hoverin oer
> Jus befo
> As we journey on our way.[347]

Drawing strength from his gathered congregation, Taylor realizes the validity of the communist imperative of collective action. In fact, the reverend achieves his greatest sense of strength while in the midst of the protesters: "Taylor looked ahead and wondered what was about to happen; he wondered without fear; as though whatever would or could happen could not hurt this many-limbed, many-legged, many-handed crowd that was he."[348] Singing God's promise in the spiritual while massed together for collective political action, Taylor senses their unified strength. As the white civic leaders acquiesce and agree to give the demonstrators food, Taylor is filled with a religious ecstasy. "A baptism of clean joy"[349] sweeps over him and his faith in God the Deliverer is affirmed, for Taylor's God is one who shows His strength in the arms and legs of His active children and who delivers upon His promises of liberation. "Fire and Cloud" ends on this hopeful note of baptizing "clean joy" as all the institutions of Jim Crow oppression seem to topple in Taylor's tear-filled eyes. This new heaven and earth can be accomplished when the black church at large learns the same lesson that Taylor has learned via Lenin, "Freedom [economically, politically, *and* spiritually] belongs t the strong!"[350]

---

[347] *Uncle Tom's Children*, 178.
[348] Ibid, 179.
[349] Ibid
[350] Ibid, 180.

Uncle Tom's Children originally concluded with this Marxist benediction, but Wright amended the collection to emphasize the black church and the CPUSA's common goals of liberation by concluding with "Bright and Morning Star." Aunt Sue's heroic sacrifice at the story's conclusion is made possible only by the new dispensation of communism, which converts her Christian endurance into a political commitment to overturning Jim Crow. Aunt Sue grew up in the bosom of the black church, "feeling buoyed with a faith beyond this world," and she had viewed "the cold white mountain" of Southern racial oppression as "a part of the world God had made in order that she might endure it and come through all the stronger."[351] It was in this spirit of perseverance—akin to the stamina O'Connor felt was necessary after a redemptive encounter with Christ to endure the trials and tribulations of this life—that Sue formerly sang the spirituals, particularly "The Lily of the Valley."

Before her conversion to the CPUSA, Sue often sang in moments of depression or during hard labor.

> Hes the Lily of the Valley, the Bright n Mawnin Star
> Hes the Fairest of Ten Thousan t ma soul...
> He walks wid me, He talks wid me
> He tells me Ahm His own...[352]

She was convinced of God's love and her own self-worth. These assurances provided her with the strength to endure the injustices of the Jim Crow South because her tribulations would be forgotten after her heavenly union with Christ. But Aunt Sue's convictions change, and her faith dramatically alters as she accepts her sons' "new and terrible vision,"[353] which results from their

---

351 Ibid, 184.
352 Ibid, 181-82.
353 Ibid, 184.

communist commitment. Wright underscores the religious intensity of Sue's new faith by describing it in the Christian rhetoric of the black church.

> [D]ay by day her sons had ripped from her startled eyes her old vision, and image by image had given her a new one, different, but great and strong enough to fling her into the *light of another grace*. The wrongs and sufferings of black men had taken the place of Him nailed to the Cross; the meager beginnings of the party had become *another Resurrection*; and the hate of those who would destroy her *new faith* had quickened in her a hunger to feel how deeply her new strength went[354] (emphasis added).

In *Wise Blood*, Hazel Motes is O'Connor's invocation of the New Testament's Saul/Paul who responds to his conversion with a furious introspection, subjecting himself to scourges of the flesh to atone for his spiritual unworthiness. Hazel's faith turns his vision violently inward, and he studies his soul and to make the refinements necessary for salvation. On the contrary, Sue learns, like Dan Taylor, that God can be found in politicized groups of people. Her faith demands that she focus upon her fellow sufferers in an unjust economic/social system and forsake her previous other-worldly musings to devote her full strength to the CPUSA's this-worldly objectives. In Sue's new belief system, Jesus' assurance in Revelation 22:16 that He is "the root and the off-spring of David, and the bright and morning star" is subsumed within her certainty that the CPUSA will instigate a political revolution that will fulfill Revelation's apocalyptic vision.

The courage and conviction inspired in her by this "new and terrible vision" allow Sue to confront white oppression, even in her own kitchen. When the white sheriff and his deputies barge into her house looking for her son, Johnny-boy, they find no

---

[354] Ibid, 185.

obsequious old black nanny but a proud woman willing to make any sacrifice for her new faith. As she tells the sheriff, "White man, don yuh Anty me!"[355] For her resistance, Sue is beaten unconscious. What sustains Sue during her first confrontation with white vigilantes is the "grace" bestowed upon her by her new "faith."[356] The depth of her new faith is demonstrated even more fully when she out-races Booker, the white traitor of the communist cause, to the clearing where Johnny-boy is being tortured. She must get there first to ensure that Booker does not reveal the party membership to the sheriff, and once she gets to the clearing, Sue acts with the resolve of a determined martyr.

Sue does not pursue vengeance for her beating or even for her son's life. In her mind, Johnny-boy has already been sacrificed for the greater good of the party; likewise, she will sacrifice herself for a new heaven on earth — the racial and social equality promised by the CPUSA. Sue arrives at her fatal confrontation with a shotgun wrapped in a sheet, telling the white vigilantes it is a shroud for her son.[357] After she kills Booker and is shot herself, Sue feels her life slowly ebbing away, and Wright again closes with a Marxist benediction. Through her sacrificial death, Sue is "focused and pointed..., buried in the depths of her star, swallowed in its peace

---

[355] Ibid, 194.

[356] Ibid, 206.

[357] In *Black Boy*, Wright recounts a similar story he heard in his childhood "of a Negro woman whose husband had been seized and killed by a mob It was claimed that the woman vowed she would avenge her husband's death and she took a shotgun, wrapped it in a sheet, and went humbly to the whites, pleading that she be allowed to take her husband's body for burial. It seemed that she was granted permission to come to the side of her dead husband while the whites, silent and armed, looked on. The woman...knelt and prayed, then proceeded to unwrap the sheet; and, before the white men realized what was happening, she had taken the gun from the sheet and had slain four of them, shooting at them from her knees" (83).

and strength."[358] Sue's conversion is complete as the former devout believer and churchgoer, now communist activist, no longer identifies the "Bright and Morning Star" with the Christ of Revelation but with the red star of communism.

While the 1938 version of *Uncle Tom's Children* garnered Wright a large national audience and a lucrative publishing contract, that incarnation of the collection left him unsatisfied, feeling as if he let his white readers escape through the emotional loophole of pity.[359] Wright felt that characters such as Big Boy, Mann, and Silas could easily elicit a condescending charity from white readers. Even Reverend Taylor might be misread by a white audience as a heroic example of a Southern black who endured. Instead of functioning as the hallmark of a newly politicized black church's struggles for economic and social equality, Taylor possibly might be made to reinforce stereotypical (and wishful) depictions of extraordinarily patient Southern blacks who wear down kind-hearted but tradition-bound Southern whites. However, there is no mistaking the call to action of "Bright and Morning Star."

The revised *Uncle Tom's Children* assured Wright that the white South would have to confront his work without pity. Yet even without the escape of sympathy, few critics have followed his apocalyptic vision of a politically committed black church toward "the place where the different paths of [African-American society's] religious-centered culture...and its need for a working-class political vision can meet."[360] While Wright explored the violence resulting from African-American resistance, the white South remained absorbed in its dominant religiosity: either demanding a violent submission to Christ's call to sinners, a

---

[358] *Uncle Tom's Children*, 215.

[359] Wright, "How 'Bigger' Was Born," 31.

[360] Thomas Larson, "A Political Vision of Afro-American Culture: Richard Wright's 'Bright and Morning Star,'" 158.

submission documented in Flannery O'Connor's *Wise Blood*, or to propagating its racist gospel, which is critiqued in *Light in August*.

CHAPTER SIX:

"I TAKE MY TEXT AND I TAKE MY TIME": THE PROMISE OF INTERTEXTUAL READING (BIBLICAL OR OTHERWISE)

[W]e shall often find that not only the best, but the most individual parts of [a writer's] work may be those in which the dead poets, his ancestors, assert their immortality most vigorously.
— T. S. Eliot

The ugly fact is that books are made out of books. The novel depends for its life on the novels that have been written.
— Cormac McCarthy

ALAN NADEL MAINTAINS that "literary allusions...are a covert form of literary criticism, in that they force us to reconsider the alluded-to text and request us to alter our understanding of it."[361] And

---

[361] Alan Nadel, "Translating the Past: Literary Allusions as Covert Criticism," 650.

therein lies possibly the greatest benefit (and responsibility) of an intextual criticism, to continually adjust and refine our perceptions of texts, to read and re-read with a new vision. For instance, in each of the biblical intertexts within *Wise Blood*, *Light in August*, *Moses, Man of the Mountain*, and *Uncle Tom's Children*, we are forced to re-examine the ways in which the Bible has been read in the South. Different reading communities produce different readings, and we, as readers, must be aware of the different uses made of a common intertext. O'Connor, Faulkner, Hurston, and Wright all appeal to a common, preceding text, but each invokes the Bible from very different vantage points and for very different reasons. Leonard Orr reminds us that

> Sources of a literary text, allusions, quotations, references, epigraph and so on, result in a retextualization, the creation of an essentially new text out of the old since the old text is resemanticized or changed in function through its placement in the new text, the text that surrounds it, and because of the difference in the reading community coming upon the text in a new context.[362]

The Bible has often been viewed by the white South as a transparent text, a work whose readily detectable concerns with sin and salvation are apparent to anyone who opens its covers. On the contrary, the Bible, for the Black church, as Theophus H. Smith reminds us, has been a transformative text which not only promises deliverance but has actually helped to accomplish greater social freedom.[363] Considering the Bible and its attendant institutions as intertexts within the works of black and white Southern authors causes us to "reconsider" and "alter our understanding" of key aspects of the South's black and white

---

[362] Leonard Orr, "Intertextuality and the Cultural Text in Recent Semiotics," 815-16.

[363] Theophus H. Smith, *Biblical Formations of Black America*, 134.

religiosities: within the context of Southern race relations, who is allowed to interpret the Scriptures and in what manner?

To answer these questions, we must train ourselves to become a "text archeologist" — one who looks beneath the focused text's levels of signification to recover the intertext's "evocative potential."[364] This potential is most fully realized when intertexts are not conceived narrowly as only one literary work borrowing from another (allusion) but also as appropriations, tropes, parodies, criticisms, or endorsements of text-like webs of social signification. That is, as text-archeologists, we should pay careful attention not only to the referentiality among literary texts but also to a literary text's negotiations with its culture; what might be considered its sometimes nurturing, sometimes antagonistic surroundings, the "collection of signifying practices in a society."[365] When we join together investigations of intertexts and the focused text's surrounding culture, "texts are immediately shown to be more profoundly integrated into their originating society."[366] To take but one example, think of the untapped riches available for students of American literature if we search for as yet unheard echoes within our national literature if we follow Toni Morrison's call to investigate "the ways in which a nonwhite, Africanist presence and personae have been constructed — invented — in the United States, and of the literary uses this fabricated presence has served."[367]

Literary works "are never mere 'memories,' they rewrite what they remember."[368] O'Connor, Faulkner, Hurston, and Wright all quite conspicuously "rewrite" key biblical passages as each wrestles with the white South's intertwined gospel of race and

---

[364] Udo J. Hebel, "Towards a Descriptive Poetics of Allusion," 140.

[365] Thaïs Morgan, "The Space of Intertextuality," 246.

[366] Orr, "Intertextuality and the Cultural Text," 819.

[367] Toni Morrison, *Playing in the Dark: Whiteness and Literary Imagination*, 90.

[368] Laurent Jenny, "The Strategy of Form," 37.

religion. Even O'Connor, who at first glance does not seem to rewrite the Bible, engages in an intertextual practice sanctioned by the white South's dominant religiosity. This dominant mode of biblical interpretation is founded upon selected passages that are emphasized over others. By carefully excavating the many layers of *Wise Blood's* biblical intertexts, the careful text archeologist finds that O'Connor is employing a type of exhortative intertextuality which highlights how her revered biblical appropriations appeal to a venerated work in an effort to lend credence to and authorize the assumptions of Southern evangelical Christianity. *Light in August* revoices stories of Ham's supposed curse and Christ's passion to reveal the communal sanctioning of Christmas's racially motivated lynching. *Moses, Man of the Mountain* recasts the Exodus story of Israelite liberation to exhort African-Americans to construct a community that does not replicate the white South's racial violence. *Uncle Tom's Children*, "Bright and Morning Star" in particular, revoices the Bible's apocalyptic passages to encourage an increased, collective political commitment from black church congregations.

By studying its intertexts, a focal text is no longer isolated from the cultural, historical matrix which shaped that particular work and which it helped to shape. For Southern studies in particular, intertextual reading can provide a framework for discussing the South's distinctive culture and its impact upon the region's literature while providing a structure for examining the largely overlooked interactions between Southern black and white writers. Readers of Southern literature might then, like our fictive predecessor, Quentin Compson from *Absalom, Absalom!*, be able to create a more complete narrative from "the rag-tag and bob-ends of old stories" that make up the South's story. To be sure, the composite narrative produced in the iron cold Harvard dorm room reflects the lacunae of its co-creators, but, at its best, the resurrected narrative of Thomas Sutpen does offer a (somewhat qualified) answer to the command to "tell about the South." Quentin Compson is our redactor of the story of a man who "abrupts" upon Jefferson one day in 1833, and the "texts" which he works from are the ones passed down by his father, Miss Rosa Coldfield and the region's stories of race, violence, and a faded planter aristocracy. Each narrative is prejudiced, but taken together, while not complete, they do offer a fuller picture of Sutpen's failed dream. In fact, from the two previous redactors, Miss Rosa and his father, Quentin (with the help of Shreve) creates a completely new text.

Generating these types of new texts should be one of our goals as readers and teachers of American literature, in general, and Southern literature, in particular. We must operate under the assumption that "texts may possess knowledge collectively that single texts alone do not seem to possess."[369] The result of *Wise Blood, Light in August, Moses, Man of the Mountain,* and *Uncle Tom's Children* each revoicing biblical intertexts is the creation of a new text in the reader's mind. And the re-visioning process can be further traced throughout successive generations of authors who concern themselves with the American South—before turning his attention to the Southwest, who other than Cormac McCarthy invests poor white Southerners' struggles with more philosophical/moral urgency since Flannery O'Connor? Who among our current writers is a better reader of and respondent to Faulkner than Toni Morrison? Who but Alice Walker "rediscovered" Zora Neale Hurston and her rich legacy for African-American literature and folklore? And who signified more eloquently on Richard Wright than Ralph Ellison?

> He who has eyes, let him see.
> He who has ears, let him hear.

---

[369] Charles Vandersee, "American Parapedagogy for 2000 and Beyond: Intertextual, International, Industrial Strength," 413.

BIBLIOGRAPHY

Allen, William. "The Cage of Matter: The World as Zoo in Flannery O'Connor's *Wise Blood.*" *American Literature* 58 (May 1986): 256-70.

Archer, Emily. "'Stalking Joy': Flannery O'Connor's Accurate Naming." *Religion and Literature* 18 (Summer 1986): 17-30.

Bacon, Jon Lance. "A Fondness for Supermarkets: *Wise Blood* and Consumer Culture." *New Essays on Wise Blood.* Michael Kreyling, editor. New York: Cambridge University Press, 1995.

_____. *Flannery O'Connor and Cold War Culture.* New York: Cambridge University Press, 1993.

Bailey, Kenneth K. *Southern White Protestantism in the Twentieth Century.* New York: Harper & Row, 1964.

Bailey, Thomas Pierce. *Race Orthodoxy in the South.* New York: Neale Publishing Company, 1914.

Baker, Houston. *Blues, Ideology, and Afro-American Literature: A Vernacular Theory.* Chicago: University of Chicago Press, 1984.

Barthes, Roland. "Theory of the Text." Ian McLeod, translator. *Untying the Text: A Post-Structuralist Reader.* Robert Young, editor. Boston: Routledge & Kegan Paul, 1981.

Bleikasten, Andre. "The Heresy of Flannery O'Connor." *Critical Essays on Flannery O'Connor.* Melvin J. Friedman and Beverly L. Clark, editors. Boston: G. K. Hall, 1985.

_____. *The Ink of Melancholy: Faulkner's Novels from The Sound and the Fury to Light in August.* Bloomington: Indiana University Press, 1990.

Blotner, Joseph. *Faulkner: A Biography.* One volume edition. New York: Vintage Books, 1991.

_____. *William Faulkner's Library: A Catalogue.* Charlottesville: University Press of Virginia, 1964.

Boles, John B. "The Discovery of Southern Religious History." *Interpreting Southern History.* John B. Boles, editor. Baton Rouge: Louisiana State University Press, 1987.

Bowden, Henry Warner. "Samuel Porter Jones." *Encyclopedia of Religion in the South.* Samuel S. Hill, editor. Macon GA: Mercer University Press, 1984.

Brinkmeyer, Robert. *The Art and Vision of Flannery O'Connor.* Baton Rouge: Louisiana State University Press, 1989.

Brooks, Cleanth. "Faulkner's Ultimate Values." *On the Prejudices, Predilections, and Firm Beliefs of William Faulkner.* Baton Rouge: Louisiana State University Press, 1987.

Cash, W. J. *The Mind of the South.* New York: Random House, 1991.

Coffee, Jessie. *Faulkner's Un-Christlike Characters: Biblical Allusions in the Novels.* Ann Arbor: UMI Research Press, 1983.

Cone, James H. "Black Theology as Liberation Theology." *African American Religious Studies: An Interdisciplinary Anthology.* Gayraud Wilmore, editor. Durham: Duke University Press, 1984.

_____. *God of the Oppressed.* New York: Seabury Press, 1975.

Culler, Jonathon. "Presupposition and Intertextuality." *Modern Language Notes.* 19 (1976): 1380-96.

Davies, Horton. "Anagogical Signals in Flannery O'Connor's Fiction." *Thought* 55 (1980): 428-38.

Davis, Thadious. *Faulkner's "Negro": Art and the Southern Context.* Baton Rouge: Louisiana State University Press, 1983.

Desmond, John F. *Risen Sons: Flannery O'Connor's Vision of History.* Athens: Univesity of Georgia Press, 1987.

Dunjee, Roscoe and Carl Murphy. "Negro Editors on Communism: A Symposium of the American Negro Press." Reprinted in *August Meier & Elliott Rudwick's Black Protest Thought in the Twentieth-Century.* New York: Bobbs-Merrill, 1971.

Duvall, John N. "Murder and the Communities: Ideology In and Around *Light in August.*" *Novel: A Forum on Fiction* 20 (1987): 101-20.

Eliot, T. S. "Tradition and the Individual Talent." *Contemporary Literary Criticism: Literary and Cultural Studies.* Second edition. Robert Con Davis and Ronald Schleifer, editors. New York: Longman, 1989.

Ellison, Ralph. "Change the Joke and Slip the Yoke." *Shadow and Act.* New York: Random House, 1986.

_____. "Remembering Richard Wright." *Going to the Territory.* New York: Random House, 1986.

_____. "The World and the Jug." *Shadow and Act.* New York: Random House, 1972.

Engels, Frederick. "On the Early History of Christianity." *On Religion. Karl Marx and Frederick Engels*. New York: Schocken Books, 1964.

Fadiman, Regina K. *Faulkner's Light in August: A Description and Interpretation of the Revisions*. Charlottesville: University Press of Virginia, 1975.

Fabre, Michel. *The Unfinished Quest of Richard Wright*. Isabel Barzun, translator. William Morrow & Company: New York, 1973.

Faulkner, William. *Light in August*. New York: Vintage, 1972.

_____. *Lion in the Garden: Interviews with William Faulkner*. James B. Meriwether and Michael Millgate, editors. Lincoln: University of Nebraska Press, 1968.

Feeley, Kathleen, S. S. N. D. *Flannery O'Connor: Voice of the Peacock*. New Brunswick NJ: Rutgers University Press, 1972.

Felder, Cain H. "The Bible, Re-Contextualization, and the Black Religious Experience." *African American Religious Studies: An Interdisciplinary Anthology*. Gayraud Wilmore, editor. Durham: Duke University Press, 1989.

_____. "Race, Racism, and the Biblical Narratives." *Stony the Road We Trod: African-American Biblical Interpretation*. Cain Hope Felder, editor. Minneapolis: Fortress Press, 1991.

Fickens, Carl. *God's Story and Modern Literature*. Philadelphia: Fortress Press, 1985.

Fickett, Harold (text) and Douglas R. Gilbert (photographs). *Flannery O'Connor: Images of Grace*. Grand Rapids: Eerdmans, 1986.

Flynt, Wayne J. "One in the Spirit, Many in the Flesh: Southern Evangelicals." *Varieties of Southern Evangelicalism*. David E. Harrell, editor. Macon GA: Mercer University Press, 1981.

Franchot, Jenny. "Invisible Domain: Religion and American Literary Studies." *American Literature*. 67/4 (December 1995): 833-42.

Fredrickson, George M. *The Black Image in the White Mind*. New York: Harper & Row, 1971.

Gates, Henry Louis, Jr. *The Signifying Monkey: A Theory of Afro-American Literary Criticism*. New York: Oxford University Press, 1988.

Genovese, Eugene. *Roll, Jordan, Roll: The World the Slaves Made*. New York: Random House, 1974.

Gentry, Marshall Bruce. *Flannery O'Connor's Religion of the Grotesque*. Jackson: University Press of Mississippi, 1986.

Giannone, Richard. *Flannery O'Connor and the Mystery of Love*. Urbana: University of Illinois Press, 1989.

Gilroy, Paul. *The Black Atlantic: Modernity and Double Consciousness.* Cambridge: Harvard University Press, 1993.

Girard, René. *Violence and the Sacred.* Patrick Gregory, translators. Baltimore: Johns Hopkins University Press, 1977.

Gossett, Louise Y. "Flannery O'Connor." *The History of Southern Literature.* Louis D. Rubin, Jr., et. al, editors. Baton Rouge: Louisiana State University Press, 1985.

Gravely, Will B. "The Rise of African Churches in America: (1786-1822): Re-Examining the Contexts." *African-American Religious Studies: An Interdisciplinary Anthology.* Gayraud Wilmore, editor. Duke University Press: Durham, 1989.

Green, James L. "Enoch Emery and His Biblical Namesakes in *Wise Blood.*" *Studies in Short Fiction* 10 (1973): 417-19.

Grisset, Michel. "Introduction: Faulkner Between the Texts." *Intertextuality in Faulkner.* Michel Grisset and Noel Polk, editors. Jackson: University Press of Mississippi, 1985.

Gwynn, Frederick and Joseph Blotner, editors. *Faulkner in the University: Class Conferences at the University of Virginia, 1957-1958.* Charlottesville: University of Virginia Press, 1959.

Hale, Grace Elizabeth. *Making Whiteness: The Culture of Segregation in the South, 1890-1940.* New York: Pantheon, 1998.

Harrell, David Edwin, Jr. "Introduction." *Varieties of Southern Evangelicalism.* David E. Harrell, Jr., editor. Macon GA: Mercer University Press, 1981.

Harrington, Evans. "'A Passion Week of the Heart': Religion and Faulkner's Art." *Faulkner and Religion.* Doreen Fowler and Ann J. Abadie, editors. Jackson: University Press of Mississippi, 1991.

Harris, Trudier. *Exorcising Blackness: Historical and Literary Lynching and Burning Rituals.* Bloomington: Indiana University Press, 1984.

Headon, David. "'Beginning To See Things Really': The Politics of Zora Neale Hurston." *Zora in Florida.* Steve Glassman and Kathryn Lee Seidel, editors. Orlando: University of Central Florida Press, 1991.

Hebel, Udo J. "Towards a Descriptive Poetics of Allusion." *Intertextuality.* Heinrich F. Plett, editor. New York: Walter de Gruyter, 1991.

Hemenway, Robert. *Zora Neale Hurston: A Literary Biography.* Urbana: University of Illinois Press, 1977.

Hengel, Martin. *The Pre-Christian Paul.* Philadelphia: Trinity Press, 1991.

Hill, Samuel S. *The South and the North in American Religion.* Athens: University of Georgia Press, 1980.

_____. *Southern Churches in Crisis*. New York: Holt, Rinehart, & Winston, 1967.

_____. "The South's Two Cultures." *Religion and the Solid South*. Samuel S. Hill, editor. Nashville: Abingdon Press, 1972.

_____. "Survey of Southern Religious History." *Religion in the Southern States: A Historical Study*. Samuel S. Hill, editor. Macon: Mercer University Press, 1983.

Holman, C. Hugh. "The Unity of Faulkner's *Light in August*." *The Roots of Southern Writing: Essays on the Literature of the American South*. Athens: University of Georgia Press: 1972.

The Holy Bible Containing the Old and New Testaments. Authorized King James Version. Meridian: New York, 1974.

Hunt, John W. *William Faulkner: Art in Theological Tension*. Syracuse NY: Syracuse University Press, 1965.

Hurd, Myles Raymond. "Between Blackness and Bitonality: Wright's 'Long Black Song.'" *CLA Journal* 35/1 (September 1991): 42-56.

Hurston, Zora Neale. "Characteristics of Negro Expression." *Voices From the Harlem Renaissance*. Nathan Huggins, editor. New York: Oxford University Press, 1976.

_____. *Dust Tracks on a Road*. New York: Harper, 1991.

_____. "The First One." *Ebony and Topaz: A Collectaena*. Charles S. Johnson, editor. Freeport NY: Books for Libraries Press, 1971.

_____. "How It Feels to Be Colored Me." *The Norton Anthology of American Literature*. Third Edition. Volume 2. New York: W. W. Norton & Company, 1989.

_____. *Moses, Man of the Mountain*. Urbana: University of Illinois Press, 1984.

_____. *Mules and Men*. New York: Harper Perennial, 1990.

_____. *The Sanctified Church*. Berkeley: Turtle Island Press, 1983.

_____. *Seraph on the Suwanee*. New York: Harper Perennial, 1991.

_____. "Stories of Conflict." *Richard Wright: The Critical Reception*. John M. Reilly, editor. New York: Burt Franklin & Company, 1978.

Jacobs, Harriet A. *Incidents in the Life of a Slave Girl. Written by Herself.* Jean Fagan Yellin, editor. Cambridge: Harvard University Press, 1987.

Jackson, Blyden. "Some Negroes in the Land of Goshen." *Tennessee Folklore Society Bulletin*. 19 (December 1953): 103-107.

JanMohamed, Abdul. "Rehistoricizing Wright: The Psychopolitical Function of Death in *Uncle Tom's Children*." *Richard Wright*. Harold Bloom, editor. New York: Chelsea House, 1987.

Jenny, Laurent. "The Strategy of Form." *French Literary Theory Today: A Reader*. Tzvetan Todorov, editor. R. Carter, translator. London: Cambridge University Press, 1982.

Jordan, June. "Notes Toward a Black Balancing of Love and Hatred." *Civil Wars*. Boston: Beacon Press, 1981.

Jordan, Winthrop D. *White Over Black*. Chapel Hill: University of North Carolina Press, 1968.

Kennelly, Laura B. "Exhortation in *Wise Blood: Rhetorical Theory as an Approach to Flannery O'Connor. Flannery O'Connor: New Perspectives*. Sura P. Rath and Mary Neff Shaw, editors. Athens: University of Georgia Press, 1996.

Kinnamon, Keneth. *The Emergence of Richard Wright: A Study in Literature and Society*. Urbana: University of Illinois Press, 1972.

Klehr, Harvey. *The Heyday of American Communism: The Depression Decade*. New York: Basic Books, 1984.

Kreyling, Michael. Introduction to *New Essays on Wise Blood*. New York: Cambridge University Press, 1995.

Larson, Thomas. "A Political Vision of Afro-American Culture: Richard Wright's 'Bright and Morning Star.'" *Richard Wright: Myths and Realities*. New York: Garland Publishing, 1988.

Leonard, Bill J. "A Theology for Racism: Southern Fundamentalists and the Civil Rights Movement." *Southern Landscapes*. Tony Badger, Walter Edgar, and Jan Nordby Gretlund, editors. Tubingen: Stauffenburg Verlag, 1996.

Levine, Lawrence. *Black Culture and Black Consciousness: Afro-American Thought From Slavery to Freedom*. New York: Oxford University Press, 1977.

Lincoln, C. Eric. "Black Religion and the Black Church." *Black Experience in Religion*. C. Eric Lincoln, editor. New York: Anchor Press, 1974.

_____. "The Development of Black Religion in America." *African American Religious Studies: An Interdisciplinary Anthology*. Gayraud Wilmore, editor. Durham: Duke University Press, 1989.

Long, Charles H. "Interpretations of Black Religion in America." *Significations: Signs, Symbols, and Images in the Interpretation of Religion*. Philadelphia: Fortress Press, 1986.

Lorch, Thomas. "Flannery O'Connor: Christian Allegorist." *Critique* 10 (1986): 69-80.

Lowe, John. *Jump at the Sun: Zora Neale Hurston's Cosmic Comedy*. Urbana: University of Illinois Press, 1994.

_____. "Wright Writing Reading: Narrative Strategies in *Uncle Tom's Children*." *Journal of the Short Story in English* 11 (Autumn 1988): 49-74.

Marable, Manning. "Religion and Black Protest Thought in African-American History." *African American Religious Studies: An Interdisciplinary Anthology*. Gayraud Wilmore, editor. Durham: Duke University Press, 1989.

May, John R. *The Pruning Word: The Parables of Flannery O'Connor*. Notre Dame: University of Notre Dame Press, 1976.

McClain, William B. "Free Style and a Closer Relationship to Life." *Black Experience in Religion*. C. Eric Lincoln, editor. New York: Anchor Press, 1974.

McFague, Sallie. "The Parabolic in Faulkner, O'Connor, and Percy." *Religion and Literature* 15 (Spring 1983): 49-66.

McKnight, Edgar V. *The Bible and the Reader: An Introduction to Literary Criticism*. Philadelphia: Fortress, 1985.

Mencke, John G. *Mulattoes and Race Mixture*. Ann Arbor: UMI Research Press, 1979.

Mitchell, Carlton. "Seventh-Day Adventists." *Encyclopedia of Religion in the South*. Samuel S. Hill, editor. Macon: Mercer University Press, 1984.

Mitchell, Henry. "Two Streams of Tradition." *Black Experience in Religion*. C. Eric Lincoln, editor. New York: Anchor Press, 1974.

Montgomery, William T. *Under Their Own Vine and Fig Tree: The African-American Church in the South, 1865-1900*. Baton Rouge: Louisiana State University Press, 1993.

Morgan, Robert and John Barton. *Biblical Interpretation*. New York: Oxford University Press, 1988.

Morgan, Thaïs. "The Space of Intertextuality." *Intertextuality and Contemporary American Fiction*. Patrick O'Donnell and Robert Con Davis, editors. Baltimore: Johns Hopkins University Press, 1989.

Morrison, Toni. *Playing in the Dark: Whiteness and Literary Imagination*. New York: Harvard University Press, 1992.

Nadel, Alan. "Translating the Past: Literary Allusions as Covert Criticism." *The Georgia Review* 36 (Fall 1982): 639-51.

Newman, Mark. "Southern Baptists and Desegregation, 1945-1980." *Southern Landscapes*. Tony Badger, Walter Edgar, and Jan Nordby Gretlund, editors. Tubingen: Stauffenburg Verlag, 1996.

O'Connor, Flannery. *The Complete Stories*. New York: Farrar, Strauss, & Giroux, 1971.

_____. *Conversations with Flannery O'Connor.* Rosemary M. Magee, editor. Jackson: University Press of Mississippi, 1987.

_____. *The Habit of Being.* Sally Fitzgerald, editor. New York: Vintage, 1980.

_____. "The Catholic Writer in the Protestant South." *Mystery and Manners. Occasional Prose.* Sally and Robert Fitzgerald, editors. New York: Farrar, Strauss, & Giroux, 1969.

_____. "The Fiction Writer and His Country." *Mystery and Manners. Occasional Prose.* Sally and Robert Fitzgerald, editors. New York: Farrar, Strauss, & Giroux, 1969.

_____. "The Gothic in Southern Fiction." *Mystery and Manners.* Sally and Robert Fitzgerald, editors. New York: Farrar, Straus, & Giroux, 1994.

_____. "The Nature and Aim of Fiction." *Mystery and Manners. Occasional Prose.* Sally and Robert Fitzgerald, editors. New York: Farrar, Strauss, & Giroux, 1969.

_____. "Novelist and Believer." Mystery and Manners. Sally and Robert Fitzgerlad, editors. New York: Farrar, Strauss, and Girox, 1994.

_____. "On Her Own Work." *Mystery and Manners. Occasional Prose.* Sally and Robert Fitzgerald, editors. New York: Farrar, Strauss, & Giroux, 1969.

_____. "Southern Fiction." *Mystery and Manners. Occasional Prose.* Sally and Robert Fitzgerald, editors. New York: Farrar, Strauss, & Giroux, 1969.

_____. *Wise Blood. Three by Flannery O'Connor.* New York: Signet, 1983.

Orr, Leonard. "Intertextuality and the Cultural Text in Recent Semiotics." *College English* 48/8 (December 1986): 811-23.

Peterson, Thomas Virgil. *Ham and Japheth: The Mythic World of Whites in the Antebellum South.* Metuchen NJ: American Theological Library Association, 1978.

Plant, Deborah G. *Every Tub Must Sit on Its Own Bottom: The Philosophy and Politics of Zora Neale Hurston.* Urbana: University of Illinois Press, 1995.

Raboteau, Albert J. *Slave Religion: The "Invisible Institution" in the Antebellum South.* New York: Oxford University Press, 1978.

Rath, Sura P. and Mary Neff Shaw. *Flannery O'Connor: New Perspectives.* Athens: University of Georgia Press, 1996.

Robinson, Cedric J. *Black Marxism: The Making of the Black Radical Tradition.* London: Zed Press, 1983.

Rubin, Louis D. "Flannery O'Connor and the Bible Belt." *The Added Dimension: The Art and Mind of Flannery O'Connor.* Melvin J. Friedman and Lewis Lawson, editors. New York: Fordham University Press, 1966.

Schaub, Thomas Hill. *American Fiction in the Cold War.* Madison: University of Wisconsin Press, 1991.

Sheffey, Ruthe T. "Zora Neale Hurston's *Moses, Man of the Mountain*: A Fictionalized Manifesto of the Imperatives of Black Leadership." *CLA Journal* 29 (December 1985): 206-220.

Smith, H. Shelton. *In His Image, But...: Racism in Southern Religion, 1780-1910.* Durham: Duke University Press, 1972.

Smith, Theophus H. *Conjuring Culture: Biblical Formations of Black America.* New York: Oxford University Press, 1994.

Spillers, Hortense J. "Moving on Down the Line: Variations on the African-American Sermon." *The Bounds of Race: Perspectives on Hegemony and Resistance.* Dominick LaCapra, editor. Ithaca: Cornell University Press, 1991.

Stephens, Martha. *The Question of Flannery O'Connor.* Baton Rouge: Louisiana State University Press, 1973.

Stepto, Robert B. *From Behind the Veil: A Study of Afro-American Narrative.* Chicago: University of Illinois Press, 1979.

Sullivan, Nell M. "Persons in Pieces: Race and Aphanisis in *Light in August.*" *Mississippi Quarterly* 49/3 (1996): 497-518.

Sundquist, Eric J. *Faulkner: The House Divided.* Baltimore: Johns Hopkins University Press, 1983.

_____. "Faulkner, Race, and the Forms of American Fiction." *Faulkner and Race: Faulkner and Yoknapatawpha, 1986.* Doreen Fowler and Ann J. Abadie, editors. Oxford: University Press of Mississippi, 1987.

Thompson, Edgar T. "God and the Southern Plantation System." *Religion and the Solid South.* Samuel S. Hill, editor. Nashville: Abingdon Press, 1972.

Touchstone, Blake. "Planters and Slave Religion in the South." *Masters and Slaves in the House of the Lord: Race and Religion in the American South, 1740-1870.* Lexington: University Press of Kentucky, 1988.

Trotman, James C. "Our Myths and Wright's Realities." *Richard Wright: Myths and Realities.* C. James Trotman, editor. Garland Publishing: New York, 1988.

Turner, Darwin T. *In a Minor Chord: Three Afro-American Writers and Their Search for Identity.* Carbondale: Southern Illinois University Press, 1971.

Vandersee, Charles. "American Parapedagogy for 2000 and Beyond: Intertextual, International, Industrial Strength." *American Literary History.* 6/3 (Fall 1994): 409-433.

Walker, Alice. "Dedication—On Refusing to Be Humbled by Second Place in a Contest You Did Not Design: A Tradition by Now." *I Love Myself When I Am Laughing.* Alice Walker, editor. New York: Feminist Press, 1979.

Washington, Joseph R., Jr. "The Peculiar Peril and Promise of Black Folk Religion." *Varieties of Southern Evangelicalism.* David E. Harrell, editor. Macon GA: Mercer University Press, 1981.

_____. "Folk Religion and Negro Congregations: The Fifth Religion." *African American Religious Studies: An Interdisciplinary Anthology.* Gayraud Wilmore, editor. Durham: Duke University Press, 1984.

Watts, Leon W. "Caucuses and Caucasians." *Black Experience in Religion.* C. Eric Lincoln, editor. New York: Anchor Press, 1974.

Weathersby, H. L. "Sutpen's Garden." *The Georgia Review* 21 (1967): 354-69.

Weinstein, Philip. *Faulkner's Subject: A Cosmos No One Owns.* New York: Cambridge University Press, 1992.

West, Cornel. "Religion and the Left." *Churches in Struggle: Liberation Theologies and Social Change in North America.* New York: Monthly Review Press, 1986.

Williamson, Joel. *New People: Miscegenation and Mulattoes in the United States.* New York: MacMillan, 1980.

_____. A Rage for Order: Black/White Relations in the American South Since Emancipation. New York: Oxford University Press, 1986.

Wilson, Charles Reagan. "The Religious Culture: Distinctiveness and Social Change." *Judgement and Grace in Dixie: Southern Faiths from Faulkner to Elvis.* Athens: University of Georgia Press, 1995.

Wimbush, Vincent L. "The Bible and African-Americans: An Outline of an Interpretive History." *Stony the Road We Trod: African-American Biblical Interpretation.* Cain Hope Felder, editor. Minneapolis: Fortress Press, 1991.

_____. "Biblical Historical Study as Liberation: Toward an Afro-Christian Hermeneutic." *African American Religious Studies: An Interdisciplinary*

Anthology. Gayraud Wilmore, editor. Durham: Duke University Press, 1984.

Wittenberg, Judith Bryant. "Race in Light in August: Wordsymbols and Obverse Reflections." *The Cambridge Companion to William Faulkner*. Philip M. Weinstein, editor. New York: Cambridge University Press, 1995.

Wood, Forrest G. *The Arrogance of Faith: Christianity and Race in America from the Colonial Era to the Twentieth Century*. Boston: Northeastern University Press, 1991.

Wood, Ralph C. "Where Is the Voice Coming From?: Flannery O'Connor on Race." *Flannery O'Connor Bulletin* 22 (1993-1994): 90-118.

Woodward, C. Vann. *The Strange Career of Jim Crow*. New York: Oxford University Press, 1974.

Woodward, Richard B. "Cormac McCarthy's Venomous Fiction," *The New York Times Magazine*, 19 April 1992, 31.

Wright, Richard. *American Hunger*. New York: Harper & Row, 1977.

_____. *Black Boy: A Record of Childhood and Youth*. New York: Harper & Row, 1966.

_____. "Blueprint for Negro Writing." *Voices from the Harlem Renaissance*. Nathan Huggins, editor. Oxford University Press: New York, 1976.

_____. "How 'Bigger' Was Born." Introduction to *Native Son*. New York: Penguin, 1984.

_____. *Uncle Tom's Children*. New York: Harper & Row, 1965.

INDEX